I love working with Dave. He encourages his clients to dream big and provides us with the skills to actually achieve those goals. His detailed approach to finances has taken the mystery out of building wealth and makes it fun. *i heart money* is not only a guide to managing your finances, it's a priceless handbook for living your best life.

Ngozi Paul, Actress, Ngozika Productions

Dave has helped me evaluate and refocus my life as well as set and achieve goals both personally and financially. This new perspective has projected me into the next level of living my ultimate life.

Daniel Faria, Director, Clark & Faria

Discovering what you want out of life requires reflection, internal commitment and the right financial foundation. What's unique about Dave's approach isn't just his perfect arsenal of tools that make all this hard work a ton of fun, but his financial acumen that makes your perfect life feasible. Thanks Dave for helping me get here. What an incredible difference!

Lynn Sivec, Strategic Planner

When I hired Dave Lester to help guide me with my business, I had no idea our weekly meetings would be so beneficial in all other aspects of my life.

I've run a small, successful business for almost 20 years. I was looking for a smart business coach with financial experience to help motivate me and to help my business move into a bigger and better market.

After each meeting with Dave, I feel inspired, organized, focused and disciplined. I see solutions clearly and feel my goals are attainable. I feel an incredible energy in my professional and personal life.

I can't say enough good things about Dave. His life is a perfect example of what he teaches. He is a joy to work with!

Wendy Tancock, Wendy Tancock Design

Time and Money are the two things I used to fret over. Investing today for tomorrow's future is a big responsibility in this crazy economy. Dave enabled me to create a plan and showed me how I can live BIG while still planning and saving for the future. He's taken all the pain out of the process. I feel free.

Sharon Sehdev, Vice President, Cognition LLP

i ♥ money

i ♥ money

Enhance Your Relationship with Money to Live Your Ultimate Life

David Campbell Lester

DCL
CAPITAL

ISBN: 978-0-9865256-1-2

Library and Archives Canada Cataloguing in Publication

Lester, David Campbell, 1977–
    I [heart] money / David Campbell Lester.

On t.p. [heart] appears as a heart.
ISBN 978-0-9865256-1-2

    1. Finance, Personal. 2. Money. I. Title.

HG179.L472 2010   332.024'01   C2010-901595-9

Published by
DCL Capital Press

iheartmoney.com

Cover designed by Niall Kelly
Edited by Catherine Leek of Green Onion Publishing
Interior designed and formatted by Kim Monteforte
    of WeMakeBooks.ca

Printed in Canada

This book is dedicated to
Elspeth Lynn and Lorraine Tao.
Thank you both for encouraging
me to do what I love.

ACKNOWLEDGEMENTS

I want to thank my family who have contributed so much to this book. My brother Gord helped to edit this book with a minimal amount of grumbling. I also want to thank my mom for teaching me the value of family, and my dad for teaching me the value of integrity.

PREFACE

Let me tell you a love story.

According to my mother, my first word was "Penny." As a kid I would sit in front of the TV, rolling coins for my papa—for a cut, of course. How many six-year-olds sit through *Bugs Bunny* rolling coins with a smile from ear to ear? One of my favorite games growing up was to play the Sheriff of Nottingham, where I would go around collecting taxes from all my stuffed animals. It was in the cards at an early age that I would be a Financial Coach.

I love money.

When I get paid, I sometimes check my account in the middle of the night, transfer my set amount into savings, and then sleep well knowing that it is accruing the highest level of savings I can find in the market. I look at my investment portfolio three times a day and get shivers when dividends are paid into my account on a monthly basis.

All this might sound a bit obsessive, but if you ask any high net worth individual they will tell you that they achieved their wealth by respecting their money. Your relationship with money will be one of the longest and most important ones you ever have. It will help you live the life you want to live. It should be like

Romeo and Juliet—but without the poisoning and stabbing and weeping.

This book will show you how to "love" your money and finances by utilizing strategies that increase both your self-worth and net worth, while decreasing the feeling of being overwhelmed and confused by financial matters. I will show you how to use simple practices to reduce the stress that money can bring.

TABLE OF
CONTENTS

LOVE YOUR MONEY!

Financial independence is liberating.

Taking control of your finances allows you to map out your own destiny and achieve all the financial and personal goals you can imagine. If you can dream it, you can achieve it!

Money, however, often causes a great amount of stress in people's lives. We are bombarded by messages concerning retirement, savings, credit card points, mortgages, credit ratings, etc. Many people turn away from the stress of having to deal with their finances and avoid them at all costs. This negative association with money causes many people to see money as a great inconvenience. Some cultures consider it impolite to publicly discuss personal finances.

I, on the other hand, LOVE money.

Growing up, I wasn't imprinted with the negative associations that people can have with money. Instead, I am always thinking about what is best for my money, and this attitude has been very profitable for me financially and personally.

It is human nature to avoid things that we do not want to do. This is called procrastination. People put off doing things because they don't think they know how to do them, or because it seems overwhelming to do them. Sometimes they do things they know how to do first, but then never get around to doing what they should

1

have been doing. Procrastination is often caused by misconceptions or old beliefs learned during childhood that hold us back from our true potential. This book will show you how to slay these personal "gremlins" and live a life based on your core values while being financially sound.

Helping people overcome feelings of being overwhelmed by money problems and motivating people to go after personal goals is what I do best! While working at Merrill Lynch and BMO Financial Group I encountered many clients who all seemed to face the same challenges. They never sat down and thought out a strategy towards their money: how to spend it, how to save it, how to share it. They lived the way most of the population lives. They spent their earnings until the account was empty, charged up their credit cards knowing that another paycheck was on the way, but then never paid off their credit card balances. They spent money when they felt badly about something, or bought something that they could not afford as a way to deal with boredom. They would have all of their equity in their house, make the minimum payments on credit lines and credit cards, lease new cars every few years, and contribute the minimum to their retirement savings, while letting bankers or investment specialists figure out the details. The real problem was that they did not have a personal relationship with their money.

According to the Survey of Consumer Finances, in 2007 the mean credit card balance for families that have credit cards was $7,300 and the median was $3,000. Both numbers were up from 2004. And they'll almost certainly be up again in 2012 when the next survey is due to come out. On the other hand, only 53% of U.S. households own at least one retirement account or 401K and the median balance of a retirement savings account was only $45,000. If you deduct the debts from the median retirement savings account balances, we are a nation of people who cannot afford to retire. We really need to work off these debts and save for the future in a substantial way.

This book is intended to show you my philosophies and strategies for saving and growing personal financial wealth. You should know, however, that I am not currently working at a bank or investment brokerage. I have owned and may still own the stocks named in this book. The examples using specific stocks are meant to demonstrate the investment strategies. They are not endorsements for specific stocks. I do not take responsibility for any of the stocks named in this book, or for the changing realities of the market. You should always do your own research before investing, and you assume all market risk.

So let's get started. Let's see what your idea of wealth looks like and make plans to get you there. And remember:

The more you love your money,
the more there will be to love.

1
LOVE YOUR MONEY

Your relationship with money is one of the most important ones you will have in your life, and you should treat it like any other. You should always be respectful, thoughtful, and caring towards your money. You should take interest in its welfare. It should never be treated as a trophy or a dirty little secret. Be interested in your money. Where is it? What is it doing? What color of underwear is it wearing today?

It starts with the way you carry your money. Do you keep it all bunched up in your pants or wallet? Do you go commando (not carry any at all)? I fold mine up neatly, the same side up, in a fancy money clip.

Do you waste your money on little things? Do you make sure you get the correct change from a vendor? Do you make sure idle money is making the highest interest rate possible? Do you pick it up on the street if you see it, or walk an extra block to your bank to avoid the service fees charged when using another bank's ATM? These may seem like small things, but they are all clear indications of how you view money. Simply put, people who respect their money end up with a whole lot more of it.

People who respect their money end up with a whole lot more of it.

5

Debt, on the other hand, is like a tawdry affair that can only harm your relationship with money. Sure, it may seem exciting to use credit to buy things you cannot afford, or things that you don't even really want, but eventually the debt will catch up with you. That sweater you charged (that didn't really fit but you bought anyway because it was on sale) may end up costing twice as much because you didn't pay off the balance on your credit card.

The basic idea of this book is that paying closer attention to money gets you closer to a better life. Every dollar saved on something that I didn't really want, or need, can be contributed towards something that will truly make me happy. What makes you truly happy? It may be a bigger, better material thing, like a car, a tastier dinner with family, a more desirable vacation, or the security of a more comfortable retirement. Discretionary spending and saving can lead to a freer, more fulfilling, and happier life. A sweater that you never wear sitting at the back of your closet with the tags still on will not get you scuba diving around the Greek islands—but a dividend paying investment might!

SIMPLIFY YOUR FINANCIAL LIFE

In life we have a lot of pressures. They come at us via the sensational media, the constant bombardment of advertising that tugs at our insecurities, and from work peers, family, and friends. And then, of course, there are the expectations we place on ourselves. It can all be a bit overwhelming. Being cognizant of these pressures is the first step.

The second step is to jettison as many non-essential parts of our lives as possible. As the French writer, Antoine de Saint Exupéry, writes, "perfection is achieved, not when there is nothing more to add, but when there is nothing left to take away." A streamlined life is more manageable, less stressful, and happier. Harnessing those lost dollars spent frivolously can make a huge contribution to your retirement, or pay for a summer on the French Riviera.

Think of driving your car. When driving, where you look is where the car heads. The same is true in life—where we keep our focus is the direction our lives go. If our concentration is divided among several areas, or bogged down by items that are not our primary focus, we will not move in the right direction. We will crash into the tree of distraction.

Instead, we want to keep our sights on our primary objectives and this will help us achieve them more quickly. When we concentrate our energies on a defined set of objectives, like a "to do" list, we itemize what we need to achieve, and this makes it seem more doable than a vague list that can seem overwhelming. Purging our list of things that are of secondary importance helps us zone in and concentrate our efforts in a much more powerful and effective way.

I want you to focus on your finances. To truly love something, you need to know it. You should know exactly how much money you have, how much you make, and how much you owe. Look at all your bills and statements. What are your monthly fixed costs, such as rent or insurance, and what are your variable costs, such as eating out? Now, what expenses can you easily live without? What can you take away? How much do you make and how can you make more? The goal is to have a simple financial life.

Money is Power

I like to think of money as a powerful tool that can help me do and buy all the things that I want. To provide for me the freedom to travel, a sense of achievement when I get better as an equestrian, the feeling of joy when I share amazing dinners with great friends and family. All the things that make me truly happy. It gives me personal power – and it will for you too.

The most sensitive subject that my clients are hesitant to talk about is credit card debt. It is amazing to see how far people will go to avoid talking about it. If you do have credit card debt and it makes you cringe to think about the 18% interest accruing each month, imagine all of the relief and power you will gain back when the cards are paid off. Think what effect the cards have over you right now and how your power would all come flowing back when the debt was gone. What a release that would be!

Power also comes from having a whack of cash in your account. Knowing that you could use the money to travel or support yourself if you lost your job. The money could really help someone out if they needed it or the money could get you out of a bad relationship if you were in one. Build up a large amount of cash and see how you start to feel. Knowing you have all that cash gives you options. And those options are a source of power.

Be like the wealthy and harness the power of the almighty buck and thrive on that confidence!

AUTOPILOT

Another way to simplify our financial lives is to make aspects of it automatic. People are creatures of habit. The most successful people connect their success to positive habits that they perform over and over again. One of the most famous self-help books is Stephen Covey's *The 7 Habits of Highly Successful People*. Actions that are done repeatedly are proven to have a substantial effect.

Automatic actions have two great benefits. The first is that any action done repeatedly will have a much greater effect than one done once or infrequently. The second is that when something is done automatically, little effort is needed to sustain it. Effort and energy saved by making your finances automatic can instead be applied to more important goals.

Some habits can be negative, like smoking, or eating when one is stressed, but it is just as easy to develop positive behaviors that benefit you. It takes only 21 days to make or break a habit. Try a fun exercise. Every night before you go to bed envision yourself being completely content the next day. Imagine yourself having the best day possible, saying "hi" to people in the street, having a great day at work, and feeling the love from your family. Imagine your intense happiness for 10 minutes before you go to bed each night for 21 days. Simply picture yourself in detail being happy every day. After the 21 days have passed, see if it makes a difference. I bet you'll catch yourself smiling while walking down the street. It seems simple but it really works. Use this method to improve yourself at work, at sports, or in any of your relationships. This includes your relationship with money.

Auto-Finance

Having your financial life on "autopilot" can build wealth and happiness over time. Savings for personal goals, such as vacations, debt repayment, and retirement savings should all come out automatically when you get paid. Investment payments can also be set up to automatically buy units, which will build up over the long term. Accelerated automatic loan payments will save you thousands of dollars in interest, and free up cash flow once you are out of debt. Your variable (everyday) spending should also be automatic. If you automatically spend only a set amount of money each week, it will help you save towards your goals and retirement.

It becomes easier the more the "main thing" becomes automatic.

Auto-Goals

You should also "automatically" plan your goals each year. This will keep your ambitions at the top of your mind. Pick a day, like

January 1st, and write out your professional, material, and personal goals for the year. What you do over and over again will pay off in the long run. "The main thing," Stephen Covey says, "is to keep the main thing the main thing." This advice becomes easier, the more the "main thing" becomes automatic.

YOUR PLATONIC FORMS

My brother always makes fun of me for applying Plato's Theory of Forms to money and shopping, but it works for me and I hope it will work for you too.

Plato believed there are two worlds. There is the perfect world of "Forms," where there is a perfect bed and a perfect chair (Plato loved furniture for some reason), and a perfect "Form" of everything. There is also the imperfect material world we live in, which is copied from the world of Forms. All chairs on earth are flawed copies of the True Form of the chair, no matter how comfy. All beds are copies of the perfect bed. The role of the philosopher is to work to understand the True Forms behind everything.

So, how does this relate to money or finance? Imagine your perfect life. Imagine your perfect relationship, career, watch, computer, car, vacation, sofa, etc. When you go out and get your perfect life, you will be living the True Form of your life. Imagine having that clarity on everything. Think how easy life would be if you knew exactly what you wanted. Think of how efficient your life would be. Think of the energy you could reapply to finding and acquiring those items, working your ideal job, and living your ideal life.

Ultimately, you are the source of your own True Forms. As Plato's teacher, Socrates instructs "Know thyself!" Socrates was the very first Life Coach.

When you can clearly see the life you want, you will be more motivated to save money towards that life. So what is that life for you? Can you picture it? Let's explore your dreams, ambitions, and desires.

LIVE LIKE YOU'RE ALREADY RICH

The best way to be rich is to start thinking and acting like you are already rich. This might sound a tad ridiculous but it works. Wealthy people always make every deal tip in their favor.

HOW THE RICH BECOME RICHER

The rich do not borrow money. They lend it. They make sure every one of their assets is returning a profit. They collect fees and commissions instead of paying them. Whenever you are making a transaction think "if I was rich, what would the ideal outcome be?" It would be in your favor old chap.

You sell when everyone is buying and buy when everyone is selling. Never use your own money if you don't have to and think of how much you can lose before you think of how much you could make. If you truly want to be a millionaire you need to model the actions and decision making of millionaires. Never envy but emulate.

The middle class is middle class because of their monetary behaviors and actions. If you want to jump to the upper-income bracket you need to change your actions to mirror the wealthy. Look at typical middle-income behavior compared to the wealthy we just mentioned. They spend every dollar they make, borrow heavily, and pay interest instead of collecting it. Banks and brokerages get rich off fees and commissions on the middle income. If you want to become rich, you need to change your behaviors.

HOW THE POOR BECOME RICHER

Ah, but changing behaviors is not an easy task. It is, in fact, quite daunting, seemingly overwhelming even, especially until we understand what's behind the behavior. Where do we begin? Let's start with a practical exercise—get it down on paper. Try Exercise 1.

EXERCISE 1

Behaviors that Limit Your Wealth

Take out a piece of paper and write down all the things you will be as a rich person.

> *Example:* *Good with money*
> *Saver*
> *Hoard capital*
> *Savvy and wise*
> *Knowledgeable about markets and business*
> *Always learning*
> *Noble*
> *Honest*

Take out a second piece of paper and write down the behaviors you will not have as a rich person.

Example: *I spend more than I make*
I owe money
Have credit card debt
No investments or growing assets
Unknowledgeable and poor with money

Now, strike a line through all of the behaviors you will no longer practice and tear up the sheet of paper. You are now going to think like a rich person, behave like a rich person, and thus live like a rich person. It is never too late to be rich. Why not start right this second? Throw the scraps of ripped up paper out and let them symbolize this moment of your transformation to being a rich person.

Write out what you are going to be as a rich person once a day for 21 days.

LIMITING BELIEFS ON MONEY

Limiting behaviors keep us stuck in middle classdom. To generate true love for money and break the old ways you need to recognize what is holding you back. These behaviors could stem from your childhood or what you learned from your peers. There are many limiting beliefs and misconceptions about money and the evil that it can bring, such as if you get money you'll have to find new friends, or that money is hard to make, or that money comes and then goes so why bother to make it? All of these beliefs keep us stagnant and prevent us from enjoying the true advantages of money. Money is a means to an end that can satisfy many of our core values like family, freedom, and adventure.

Once you have identified any limiting beliefs you might have about money, it is time to change them into enabling beliefs. Ask yourself the following questions:

- What do I gain from having this belief?
- What do I lose from having this belief?
- Why do I hang onto this belief?
- What could I have if I lost this belief?

You should now know whether the limiting belief is holding you back or not. If it is, you will need to transform it to an empowering belief. Try Exercise 2 to find that empowerment.

EXERCISE 2

Turning Limitations into Empowerment

Write down your limiting belief on a piece of paper.

Example: "I'll have to make new friends if I become rich."

Now cross out this sentence and write after it 25 times:

I deserve to be rich
I am worthy of being rich
I will be rich
I must be rich
I shall be rich
Rich is good

Do this as many times as you need to until you no longer associate with the limiting belief.

I've enabled myself to be independently wealthy at a young age by accepting my empowering belief that "If I love money it will love me back."

WHAT DOES RICH LOOK LIKE?

Absolutely anyone can have tons of money. Money never judges you by the clothes you wear or what social economic class you grew up in. You could have wretched shoes and it still wouldn't care. Money doesn't discriminate. You just have to keep an open mind and say "yes please" and take a second helping when money comes to you. I have known wonderful rich people and quite horrible ones too. The common theme among them is that they'll take money when it comes their way.

You need to decide what rich will look like to you. Many people amass huge fortunes but are never happy. From the get go be sure to decide what rich means to you. It could mean having enough money so you won't have to worry. Or rich could mean having the interest from the interest of the interest on your money cover your chosen lifestyle. Ask yourself what amount you want and then what that amount will give you.

WHAT DO THE RICH DO?

Remember that for the rich, money always makes money. Anyone who loves money knows the rule of compounding interest—$10 at 9% interest will double every 8 years. Money that pays you money and then pays more money adds up really quickly. The more money you have compounding, the more money you will make.

Remember that for the rich, money always makes money.

Know where you are financially so you can see where you are going. Take time once a week to track your total assets minus your liabilities. Taking a closer look at your budget will give you an idea where you can stop the bleeding. If you are hemorrhaging in a certain area, plug it so that you are always making more money than you are spending.

What Rich Looks Like to Sir Richard

Sir Richard Branson is a great guy. He went from being a young, middle-class English dude to being a huge entrepreneur, being knighted and changing industries—the world even. I read his autobiography a few years back and the one thing that stuck with me was his philosophy on growing his business. I found it so intriguing that I use it for my own stock trading and business development. I think it'll help you too.

Richard was in a bit of a pickle. He had sold Virgin Music to concentrate on Virgin Atlantic Airways, and British Airways was right on his back. His planes had become a bit older and he wanted to keep his superior customer experience advantage by adding the new flat-screen TVs to each chair, which BA didn't have. He went to the bank to try to borrow a huge amount—I don't remember, let's say a $200-million loan—to upgrade the planes. The bank's reply? "Computer says no."

We all know that Sir Richard doesn't stop at anything or take no for an answer, so he went back and asked for a loan for $1 billion to buy entirely new planes! At that point "Computer says yes." He got his loan and grew his company.

My main point is that we need to emulate the wealthy. The traditional approach to debt is to cut all spending and pay it down, while living on cat food and playing scrabble for ten years. That is what all of the financial guru's will tell you. Sir Richard wouldn't do that. He would ask himself, "How can I get those TVs and come out ahead again?" So ask yourself, "How can I pay off my debt and still live my life?"

Here is what I've got off the top of my head. What do you come up with?

1. Do something that you love in order to make more money.
2. Ask for more money at work.
3. Get a head hunter to get you a new, higher paying job.

4. Learn to blog and sell advertising space, like me!

Grow your way out of your financial problems and win big! Living on a restricted budget won't help you live your best life. By emulating the rich you also need to dress the part. I'm not talking about crazy gold necklaces or Maybachs, but wear the uniform of old money. Quality clothes that are understated but neat and sharp. When you look good, you'll feel good and perform well. Appearance is everything and making sure that you're making the best impression from the moment you walk into a room will help you close deals, make connections, and help you blend in with other wealthy folk. Dress the part and soon you'll be strutting the strut.

Think about what you have that others might need. It is hard to become rich working for someone else and you'll need to discover what you have to offer the world. When working for yourself you have an instinctive drive to better yourself. Make your talents benefit you instead of a corporation. Many very rich people ventured out on their own to create their own empires. Take action to benefit yourself. Decide where there is a need and satisfy it with your talent or skill. Every step towards your own financial abundance is a step closer to being rich. Who is better to sell your skills than you? Learn to sell your own skill or talent and you will be halfway to your own business.

Identifying the disconnects between what we want and how we behave allows us to learn a little about what we want from life. But we need a clearer picture if we are really going to make a difference in our lives.

SETTING GOALS FOR YOUR ULTIMATE LIFE

Goals are important for establishing what we want to achieve in life. It keeps us focused, and helps us to crystallize our true objectives, as opposed to our passing fancies. We cannot buy and do everything, so this helps us to prioritize and clarify what we really want. Saving each disposable dollar towards something that we truly want will make us happier and more fulfilled people. It will also give us a sense of confidence and self-worth when our goals are achieved.

Prepare a "Goals" file folder and fill it with plans of what you want to accomplish in life. I have a goals folder from when I was in high school. It is amazing to go back and see what I was hoping to accomplish back then, check off what I have actually accomplished, and discover what my new goals look like now that I am in my thirties. I feel rewarded every time I look back at my accomplishments. Some of the goals that I achieved this past year, like visiting the ancient Minoan ruins on Crete and swimming in volcanic springs on Santorini, I had on my goals list back in 1997.

Dream Big! Think big— this is your life!

21

DREAM BIG!

Let's make your list. Run and get a pad of paper and a pen. Did you get it yet? All right, you're ready for Exercise 3.

EXERCISE 3

Personal, Professional, and Material Goals

You need three sheets of paper.

1. At the top of the first sheet write "Personal Goals."

    Brainstorm everything that you want to accomplish in your life that is of personal importance. This includes relationships you want to have or improve, educational programs, volunteering and philanthropic work, and physical challenges you want to accomplish, like yoga or an Iron Man competition.

    Think big—this is your life!

    Do not hold anything back. Let it all flow out and fill as many pages as you can, even if you feel yourself doubting anything on the list. Write down everything.

2. At the top of the second sheet write "Professional Goals."

    Now do the same thing. Open the floodgates and brainstorm every possible thing that you want to achieve in your career. Again, do not limit yourself. You are your best champion so write down everything you want to achieve. Write down if you want to change careers at a certain point in time, if you want to start your own business, go into politics, work abroad, anything that you can dream of.

    I can dream a lot so my goals folder is hefty and yours should be too.

3. At the top of the third sheet write "Material Goals."

   This is the fun one for me. Anything that you want to buy goes on this one: trips to Europe, luxury cars, art, diamonds, whatever your heart desires.

Now that you have all of your hopes and dreams brainstormed, we are going to add them to your own personal "Life Status."

LIFE STATUS

Once you have brainstormed your three goal lists in Exercise 3 we can think about them in more detail in a "Life Status." I use this with all of my clients to keep their goals organized and at the top of their minds, and we are going to make you one too.

At the top of three new sheets of paper, write "Personal Goals," "Professional Goals," and "Material Goals." Under each heading write the following subheadings: Goal, Description, Value, Priority, Due Date, Current Status, Next Step, and Cost.

An example would be organized like this:

LIFE STATUS: Personal Goals

Goal	Description	Value	Priority	Due Date	Current Status	Next Step	Cost

So let's fill these out. Go back to your three sets of Goals from Exercise 3. List the goals in the goal column under each Life Status.

Beside each goal write a brief description of what the goal is or how frequently you will perform the goal. It is important to write this down so you can clearly visualize the goal. It is also important to be specific about your goals.

For example, if you want to spend a summer in Greece on an island, first name the island, and then describe what your lifestyle would be like on the island. You might write, "I want to live on Santorini. I want to wake up and have a coffee on my patio while looking at the boats on the sea. I want to go to the beach and swim every morning. Every evening I want to have a traditional Greek meal under the stars." If you can imagine your goal in perfect detail it will be easier for you to achieve.

LIFE STATUS: Personal Goals

Goal	Description	Value	Priority	Due Date	Current Status	Next Step	Cost
Yoga	2 x Week						

Many people use vision boards for the same purpose. Every morning while having coffee they spend some time looking at images of all the things they would like in their lives. It helps to keep you focused on what you really want in life. Try it.

Go to the store and buy a whack of magazines that you love to read. Cut out any images of homes, cars, cottages, vacation spots, fashion, etc. Then place the board with all of the images somewhere you will see it every day. It is amazing how many of these things will come to you. When your brain focuses on the things that you want, it will try to help you get them. I have clients who found their partners this way. It is amazing.

Values Exercise

We each have core values through which we filter our lives. When we are not living based on our core values we generally feel unhappy or think that our lives are out of balance. Assigning a value to each goal gives us a sense of why each goal is important to us. When we are working towards one of our goals and we feel that we cannot accomplish it, it is important to go back to our goal list and remember why it was important to us in the first place. Exercise 4 will help you uncover your core values. Do this exercise with your partner to see what motivates them. It's amazing how when you know each other's values, you know each other that little bit better. When you're in disagreement, it will help to understand where each of you is coming from.

EXERCISE 4

Your Core Values

To determine your core values, take out a pad of paper and pen. Think of people in your life or from history who have characteristics that you respect.

Now, think of what specific characteristics you admire and write them down for each of the individuals that you picked.

Look at the characteristic of each character. There should be 8-10 character traits.

Now ask yourself, if you had that character trait, what values would you really possess?

Example:
Julius Caesar is someone from history that I respect. I like that he was ambitious (to say the least). If I had Caesar's ambition, what would I have? I would have success. And if I had success, what would I have? I would have confidence. And if I truly felt confident, what sense would I have? When I think long and hard about it, I would have a sense of achievement.

That exercise showed that one of my core values is achievement.

Another approach is to think about the kind of legacy you want to leave behind. How do you want to be remembered? Personally, I want to be remembered for helping as many people as I could live their dreams. To discover what value is associated with me wanting to help people, I would ask myself: "If I had helped hundreds of people live better lives by aligning their finances to their dreams what would I have?" After thinking about it for a few seconds, it comes to me that I would have a sense of contentment. And if I asked myself, "what would I have if I had contentment?" I would say that I felt like I was contributing to people's success. Then I ask myself "If I truly felt that I was contributing to people's success, what would I have?" I would have a sense of leadership. Leadership is another of my core values and it is behind my motivation to write this book and to be a Financial Coach.

How do you want to be remembered?

Work through Exercise 4 until you have 8-10 core values. Now let's go back to your Three Life Status lists and align these values (third column) with each of your Personal, Professional, and Material goals. Here is a sample list of traditional Core Values:

Respect	Wisdom
Love	Peace
Integrity	Friendship
Fun	Community
Learning	Security
Joy	Leadership
Achievement	Creativity
Balance	Freedom

LIFE STATUS: Personal Goals

Goal	Description	Value	Priority	Due Date	Current Status	Next Step	Cost
Yoga	2 x Week	Fun					

PRIORITIZE YOUR LIFE

In the Priority column, number your Personal, Professional, and Material goals from 1 to 3, with 1 being the highest priority and 3 being the lowest.

Take all of the "1" priorities and make a single goals list for this year so that it fits on one or two pages. You will get a feeling about which goals are your top priorities. Make sure that your primary goals are the ones that give you the most "goose bumps" when you imagine them.

Any goals that you can start immediately, start. Anything that you can do by picking up the phone, such as joining a gym, trying yoga, calling an old friend, or taking your parents out to a nice restaurant, you should do now. You will feel *amazing* once you have achieved your first goal. You have got many more to go.

> *Make sure that your primary goals are the ones that give you the most "goose bumps" when you imagine them.*

Putting the Plan into Action!

It is important to set a plan for each goal. For each goal ask yourself the following ten questions and write down the answers. I've used my own goal, "I want to start my own business," as the example to get you started.

1. *Is your goal achievable?* Yes, many people have started their own businesses before and I am passionate about my business.

2. *Is your goal realistic?* Yes, I have done the research and there is a demand for my services.

3. *Does your goal have a timeline?* Absolutely, my business will be open by September of this year.

4. *Is the goal specific?* Yes, I have a business plan as opposed to just saying I want to start my own business at some point and I have expressed that I want to start my own business to friends and family.

5. *Is your goal measurable?* Yes, I will know I have completed it when I am a successful business owner and have replaced my old salary.

6. *Are you super enthusiastic about your goal?* Yes, I have contacted many people who are already interested in my services. I have thought of a name and how to gather clients. My plan will be my map to success.

7. *Is the goal natural for you?* Yes, my product is amazing. I have tested interest for it, and everyone is interested.

8. *Do the people in your life understand the goal?* Yes, my family knows that this is my ideal career and supports me.

9. *Are you ready for the journey?* Yes, I realize that I need financial backing, so I have saved 1 year of salary to help me through the start up and growing part of the company. I also have a contingency plan if the business takes longer to grow.

10. *Does it give you "butterflies" when you think of achieving your goal?* Absolutely, I can't sleep thinking of how happy and fulfilled I'll be when I have my own business.

Beside the Priority column there are Current Status and Next Step columns. Some of your goals may seem a bit daunting before you start going after them, but listing the steps to get to your goals is half the battle. Truly successful people complete their most challenging goals by breaking them down into a list of "little wins."

For each goal, go to the Current Status column and think about what the first thing is that you need to do to get to your goal. Think of the easiest thing you need to do to achieve that goal.

If your goal is going to yoga twice a week, then you would price out studios. On your way home drop by a studio that has been recommended by a friend, or one near your work, and check it out. Or you could do an online search for Yoga Studios. Then celebrate that you have made the first move towards your goal; pat yourself on the back for taking the first step. The following day, write down the number of the first yoga studio and give them a call, then celebrate that you are closer to achieving your goal. After a week of baby steps, you will have called all of the studios for prices and booked your first session! There are faster ways to go to yoga, but this example shows you how to eat an elephant—bite by bite.

In the chart, be sure to write down where you are currently in achieving each goal, and write down all of the next steps. When you complete each step, add the line item from Next Steps to the Current Status column so you know what you are working on for each goal. This way you will always know where you are in regards to each goal. Do this for all of your Personal, Professional, and Material goals and it will keep you constantly moving "step by step."

LIFE STATUS: Personal Goals

Goal	Description	Value	Priority	Due Date	Current Status	Next Step	Cost
Yoga	2 x Week	Fun	1	Dec 1st	Researched studios	Sign up for class	

Goals Costing

The last column in our Life Status goal chart is Cost. Figure out how much each goal will cost, if it has a cost. Do some research to figure out the correct amount. If it is a car or a trip, surf the Internet to get an estimate.

Figure out how many months you have until you want to achieve the goal and divide the amount by the number of months. Place this amount beside each goal in the "Cost" column.

The next chapter will show you how to redirect savings towards achieving these goals.

LIFE STATUS: Personal Goals

Goal	Description	Value	Priority	Due Date	Current Status	Next Step	Cost
Yoga	2 x Week	Fun	1	Dec 1st	Researched studios	Sign up for class	$10 wk

GOALS FOLDER

Now that you have your three lists, get a file folder and place the lists inside. Whenever you read an article that is inspiring, see a picture of a place you want to visit, find a great quotation or poem, or a brochure on the car you want to buy, place it in the file folder. Review your folder at the beginning of the year to update your goals lists and to review what you have accomplished so far.

Even though we are not always consciously thinking about our goals, if we remind our subconscious what we want to achieve in the long run, it will constantly be problem solving on our behalf to achieve these goals. It is the same when we are trying to remember a piece of information; if we start working on something else, our subconscious will keep digging, and the information we were looking for just comes to us. What is more automatic than having our minds work on our behalf when we are doing our day-to-day tasks?

Whenever I am having a crappy day, I open up my Goals Folder and browse through my list of still to be accomplished goals. It takes my mind off what I am worrying about and refocuses me on what is truly important to me. This helps me work towards my long-term goals. It is amazing how well this works. In 5 years or so you will be looking at a list of accomplished goals that otherwise you might not have even attempted.

KEEPING MOTIVATED

Ask yourself the questions below when you feel less motivated. Sit for a while and wait for the answers to come to you.

1. What am I procrastinating about?
2. What belief about that goal/task/achievement is holding me back from taking the next step?
3. What fear is behind that belief?
4. If I had no chance of failing, what would be my next step?
5. What would make me most comfortable with this action/decision/situation?
6. What is my best first step to get there?
7. What would be the first step/action/solution, if I did know it?

When you feel like you need an extra little kick to get yourself moving on one of your goals, filter each goal through these questions and write down the answers. Remember that you have been through this thought process and all of these concerns have already been thought through. Remind yourself of the Core Value that you associated with each goal and how achieving that goal will make you happy.

Once you have your millions, you'll need to learn how to hold onto them. Make sure you always spend your own money. Keep responsibility over it. Respect it and it will respect you right back. It took long hard work to get it and you'll want to keep and enjoy it a long time.

BUDGETING FOR YOUR GOALS

Budgeting is the last thing most people want to do. It's close in appeal to a dentist's drill or doing your taxes. Think of budgeting as a type of mapping. It gives you directions towards the completion of your goals and dreams. This is where we prioritize what we really want out of life, and concentrate our financial and physical energies. If we do not have a financial map we will always be lost. When you control your finances, you control your destiny.

> *When you control your finances, you control your destiny.*

BUDGET BOX

Let's get organized! Buy a box with several file folders and that can fit inside a filing cabinet. I went to the local stationery store and got a really fancy box to house my goals and budget folders because it is so important to me. I have a long history with fancy boxes. When I was young I kept my important things in a velvet-lined treasure chest.

Once you have the box, you'll keep your goals and Life Status pages here along with lots of other budgeting information. Label the file folders as follows:

- Goals
- To Pay
- Phone
- Bank Accounts
- Investments
- Cable
- Electricity
- Mortgage
- Insurance
- Taxes
- Any other bill that applies to you

When a bill comes, check it to make sure there are no errors and they are not bilking you on anything, and place it in its respective folder. If any bills come that don't automatically get paid each month, place them in the "To Pay" file. When they are paid, place them in their appropriate folder. This should be the end of lost bills, piles of bills, or sock drawers full of bills that you do not want to face. You will save money that would have been wasted on late fees. Having your bills organized will also instill a sense of control over your finances. Plus, you get a fancy box!

THE ART OF BUDGETING

Most budgets are divided into two areas—fixed costs and variable costs. Fixed costs are those expenses that are consistent from month to month. Variable costs, on the other hand, can change weekly. But for our budgeting project, we are going to add two additional components—retirement savings and goal budgeting.

FIXED COST BUDGETING

For this section you will need to gather the last 3 months or more of bank and credit card statements. Write down all of your fixed costs that come out of your accounts. These include your rent or mortgage, student loans, day care costs, insurance, and car loans (and only car loans because we never lease—we will get to this later). Also include your cable, cell phone, landline, Internet, electricity bill, heating and any other costs that are charged to you every month. Write them all down by item and add up the total.

VARIABLE COST BUDGETING

Figure out how much you spend every week on things like groceries, gasoline, coffee, clothing, and eating out. The best way to determine these costs is to take a 3-month average by going through your credit card and bank account records. And don't forget to include cash, although you won't likely be able to attribute it to specific items. This will be a huge learning opportunity for you.

When I did this I learned that if I had two coffees a day at $2.05, it was costing me $4.10 a day, $20.50 a week, $82 a month, and $984 a year! Eating out for lunch at $10 a day cost $50 a week, $200 a month, and $2,400 a year. If I were to cut out coffee and lunches, I would have another $3,384 for a trip to hang out with penguins in the south of Chile or to buy three really nice suits.

Write down all of your monthly variable costs and then do the math. Figure out how much you are spending each year on those items. Good ones to watch are your total automotive costs, clothing, restaurant bills, and bar tabs. When you are looking at the yearly totals you will realize that if you eliminate, or reduce, those expenses you will have new sources of money to invest in yourself. Pump those savings back into your own happiness.

Once you've slashed back the non-essentials, take the average monthly variable cost total and divide it by four. This will give you your weekly cash allowance that you take out every Sunday night from the bank machine. This amount needs to last you until next Sunday. Here is an example of a weekly budget for a single person.

> *Pump those savings back into your own happiness.*

Weekly Budget — Single Person

Gas	$80
Groceries	$100
Lunches	$50
Clothes	$50
Coffees	$20
Total	**$300**

Therefore you are permitted to withdraw $300 only from the bank each Sunday.

Knowing that you only have $300 to spend for the week means that you will have to pay close attention to your spending. If you go over on gas and spend $100, you will know that the extra $20 will have to come from one of the other categories. If you really want some awesome boots and they are $100, you will have to save your $50 for clothes for 2 weeks to be able to afford them.

The benefit is that you have the freedom to spend the $300 how you want. If you want to go on a bender and blow the $300 Sunday night, you can. You will have to last the rest of the week, though, before you get another $300, but that would be your choice.

Weekly budgeting is the best way to simplify your finances and cut down on your discretionary spending. It will force you to think about everything you buy.

RETIREMENT SAVINGS

Retirement savings should be in everyone's budget. The rule of thumb is that 10% of your *net* pay should be placed towards your retirement each month. Figure out what your monthly take-home pay is and multiply it by 10%. This is now one of your fixed costs.

Also, calculate what your individual retirement arrangement will be and add it to the money that you will have to contribute toward your goals budget (see next section). There are many online calculators that will help you estimate this figure. Your bank's website is the best place to start looking for one.

Some companies have a contribution matching program where they match what ever you put in. You should *always* take advantage of this. If there is free money out there, take it. I love free money. Find out from your human resources department if there is an employee contribution plan and sign up for it. There may be some limitations but take advantage of what you can. Take your contributions from work into consideration when you figure out how much you will need to add in each year to get to your retirement goal.

How Much Is Enough?

To figure out how much money you will need to retire, first determine how much before-tax income you would like to receive. Many experts suggest you don't need as much salary in retirement as you do while working. I disagree. You want more! Think of all of the amazing things you want to achieve from your Life Status lists when you have the time to do them. It will be your retirement so empower yourself to make sure you know how much you will need and how to get there. The worst thing would be to get to that age and not be ready. No one wants to eat cat food during his or her golden years.

Let's say you've determined you will require $60,000 annual income upon retirement. To calculate the principal amount that you'll need to have to invest at a conservative 5% return a year:

Calculate for a 5% Return
Annual Income/Return = Investment Assets
$60,000/.05 = $1,200,000

That $1.2 million is a big number. In order to get to $1,200,000, it takes $800 invested per month for 30 years with an average return of 8%. I will show you my own strategy of having multiple streams of income, and where I recommend to invest later in the book.

Really the big thing here is to determine what your retirement will look like. It may involve many long discussions with your family. From there, figure out your desired income and then calculate how many assets paying out at 5% you will need. Be sure to add your desired amount in your Life Status for future reference.

Higher Education Savings Account (ESA)
If you have kids you should start investing for their education right away. The huge benefit of starting early is that you have an entire 18 years for your money to compound before they have to rush off to school. This compounding factor will allow small monthly donations to build into a large amount for Junior to go to school with.

To take full advantage of the 18 years, buy international dividend or select dividend Exchange Traded Funds (ETF). We know that in 18 years the Chinese and Indian economies will be the same size or larger than the North American economy and you want to participate in that growth. I want to accelerate that growth by re-investing distributions to buy more units, like I do with the Zero Effort Portfolio (later on in the book in Chapter 6). Basically, the income funds will pay monthly so you can buy more units; the following month the new units will buy more units and so on. I'm sure you can see that over 216 months this will propel Junior's education fund.

On top of the compounding interest, the government will not tax ESA earnings (up to $2,000 a year) if used for the child's qualified education expenses.

529 Plans vary by state but you can contribute up to $2,000. ESAs and 529 Plans are controlled by a responsible individual until all assets are distributed. A 529 Plan will not limit use of the Hope Scholarship Credit or lifetime Learning Credit. The account is an asset of the parent and therefore Junior may still qualify for more financial aid.

And it just keeps getting better! All income earned within an ESA is sheltered from taxes and is withdrawn tax free to pay for Junior's education at 18. Keeping it sheltered from taxes means that the compounding can really take effect. Junior will be taxed when he withdraws the funds but since he'll be in school it will likely be at the lowest rate.

Here's the math. You invest $200 a month for 18 years into the iShares International Index (IDX) or the Dow Jones Select Dividend Fund (IDV) at an annual compounding return of 8% within an ESA or 529 Plan. Re-invest the distributions and start it with $1,000. You'll have over $100,000 for Junior to go to school when he turns 18! Amazing right? If you add Nana and Auntie Gertrude's birthday money into the fund along the way you'll have even more growth.

My best strategy is to invest your monthly $200 in two iShares funds 50-50—$100 in the iShares International Select Dividend Fund and $100 in the iShares U.S. Preferred Stock Index Fund. At current prices this will give you an average 8% yield with which to buy more units. As the international and domestic market increases, you'll get some growth. Even if you don't get any growth in the next 18 years, you'll still have the 8% monthly distributions buying more units each month. Buying both iShares index funds will limit your downside, due to the stability that comes from the iShares U.S. Preferred Index Fund investing in U.S. blue chip stocks, but also allows for more upside as China, India and the world grow their economies in the iShares International Select Index Fund. That adds up to a whole lot of books for Junior!

GOAL BUDGETING

Get your Personal, Professional, and Material goals lists. Which goals will be your priorities for the year? How much will the first one cost? Divide that by 12 and write the number down on your Goal Budget. If it is not a substantial amount of money, you can add more items using the same process (total cost ÷ 12). If some of your goals are large purchases, like a cottage, then it makes sense to amortize the cost over the number of months it will take to put together a down payment or to purchase the item completely.

Dream big and budget to achieve your goals.

This system works! Dream big and budget to achieve your goals. I saved $1,000 a month for a year to pay for a trip to Europe. Last summer I spent a month visiting all of the ancient ruins and historical sites, swimming in the Santorini volcanic springs, eating pork knuckle and sauerkraut in Bavaria, living the bohemian life in trendy East Berlin, and shopping my heart out in Sweden. I love Swedish designers and their clothes fit my build perfectly.

As you complete each of your goals, the next on the priority list will be added to the goal funding equation. This process will continue until all goals with a #1 priority are achieved. Goals that do not cost anything, like reading, should still be on the list. They can be equally valuable to your happiness.

BUDGET FINALIZATION

Your budget should now have all of your fixed costs, variable costs, and goal costs. I have included a sample budget based on an after-tax monthly income of $5,000.

Monthly Budget Based on $5,000 Income

Fixed Costs	Monthly
Mortgage	$1,350
Property Tax	$100
Electricity	$30
Cable	$80
Heating	$100
Internet	$20
Car Loan 1	$350
Car Loan 2	$350
Insurance: Car/Home	$200
Retirement Savings	$500
TOTAL	**$3,080**

Variable Costs	
Groceries	$400
Gasoline	$320
Lunches	$200
Clothing	$200
Coffee	$80
Hair Cuts	$50
TOTAL	**$1,250**

Goal Costs	
Savings: Other	$135
Trip: Greece	$350

Gym × 2	$100
Mandarin Class	$35
Camera	$50
TOTAL	**$670**

This family has prioritized their goals of going to Greece, joining a gym to get into shape, taking a Mandarin language course, and buying a camera to record the trip.

As you achieve your goals you will want to achieve more. Take your lunch for a week and achieve another goal. Get coffee at work and put that money toward achieving another goal. This is your challenge: make a budget that cuts your excess spending, saves for your retirement, and finances your dreams and desires.

HOW TO USE MONEY AND CREDIT

CASH IS BACK

When talking about staying on budget, all experts tell us the same thing: use cash. Before credit cards, debit cards, and charge cards, there was good old, hard currency. The earliest examples of using precious metals as money are from the third millennium BC in Mesopotamia and Egypt. By contrast, credit cards have only been around for the last 60 years or so, and therefore cash has a pedigree that I am happy to stick with.

There are many benefits to cash. It can get us better deals when making large purchases. It is accepted more often than plastic. There is also the physicality of the money leaving your fingers when forking over a large amount of cash, as opposed to sliding a piece of plastic through a slot and thinking you don't have to pay for another 2 weeks. You should always see your money leaving when you buy something. If a purchase gives you a bad feeling, maybe you should rethink it.

If a purchase gives you a bad feeling, maybe you should rethink it.

Do not spend money unless you have it. It is important to have the cash before you drop the cash. It will make the purchase more rewarding too because you have saved for it. This will also keep you on your fixed budget, and will not throw off future monthly budgets by forcing you to take from your savings to pay for a previous month's purchase. The streamlining of your spending is dependent on you keeping to your monthly budgets.

EVERYDAY BANKING

No one needs more than two bank accounts at one bank—full stop. You need a checking account for your day-to-day banking, and just in case you need to write a check for some reason. I think the only checks I have written in the last few years have been to set up automatic deposits into my account! You will also need a high interest savings account. All of the banks offer this now. If you can find a third-party bank with higher interest rates then set up a savings account there with a link to your checking account. You can then easily have an automatic transfer set up to send money from your checking account to the high interest savings account and reap the rewards.

Try to keep the $1,500 minimum balance, or whatever is required, in the bank account at all times to avoid any monthly fee. If your monthly fee is $8.50 a month and you save that amount for 12 months, you will have saved $102 on the $1,500 in the account. That's the same as earning 7% interest on the minimum balance.

Annual Interest on Saving Bank Fees
$$\$8.50 \times 12 = \$102$$
$$\$102/\$1500 = 7\%$$

Overdraft protection should only be used in emergencies. They charge 20% interest once you withdraw from the account, plus a fee of $5 or more. If you have the suggested $1,500 minimum balance you will have a natural cushion and will not go into overdraft.

AUTOMATIC BILL PAYMENTS, SAVINGS, AND CASH WITHDRAWALS

All bill payments should be set up so that they come out of your checking account on the same day that your paycheck is deposited into your account. This will stop the annoyance of having to write checks, pay bills online individually, or forgetting to pay them and getting hit with hefty late fees.

Add up all of your expenses that need to come off your pay, such as rent or mortgage, electricity, Internet, car payments, other loans, debt repayment, cable, phone bill, cell phone bill, etc. If you are paid twice a month, split them evenly so that an equal amount comes out each payday. Savings for goal purchases will come out of your account automatically and be deposited into your savings account. This is the money that you will be using to fulfill your goals list. Things that are automatic are out of sight and out of mind.

Withdraw cash for the week on Sundays. This way you will not need to use your debit card and will avoid going over your monthly allowance and paying extra fees.

ONLINE BANKING

Check your account balances often to make sure nothing has come out of your account that should not have, and to make sure that you are being paid the correct interest on your savings balance. Banks make mistakes and you want to make sure that you are in full control of your accounts. Those bankers are sneaky, so be sure to watch them.

Remember that knowing what goes on behind the "money curtain" keeps you confident and in control of your finances. I check my accounts daily. Every penny must be accounted for or I cannot sleep at night. I have gone to the extreme of calling the bank to reverse charges if they charge me an extra $0.60 from my account! Instead of you paying service fees to the bank, they should be paying you with interest. Shouldn't the bank be paying you so they can use your deposited money? It makes a whole lot of "cents."

Knowing what goes on behind the "money curtain" keeps you confident and in control of your finances.

CREDIT CARDS

My rules for credit cards are easy. You may have them, but only use them for fixed monthly expenses or large purchases, and always make sure you have the cash to pay them in full right away.

Credit cards encourage bad financial behavior. People shop more often with credit cards, they get convinced to buy something because of all the points or cash back, they lead to paying for someone else's lunch because it's easier to throw down one card than splitting the bill, and there is no connection to our 5,000-year-old tradition of exchange—where something "precious" leaves your possession for goods or services rendered. Keep them holstered. Use cash.

Credit card interest rates and sneaky payment methods are something else that should keep you away from using your cards. Most cards have an 18% interest rate, or higher. If you buy a shirt for $10 and don't make any payments, your $10 T-shirt will have cost $22.88 after 5 years.

Look at your credit card purchases and think twice about whether everything you charged to them was worth it. Did you really need everything on that bill? Did you overspend at any time?

If you are paying interest on past due balances, are the purchases worth twice what you paid for them? Would you not rather have that extra money working for you in a high interest bank account or investment?

What's the Points?

How many points cards do you have clogging up your wallet? When was the last time you actually went on a free trip or got some sort of reward from them? Have you ever determined how much more money you spend traveling across town to use that store or extra dollars you put on your credit cards to get a few more points?

Due to the fact that I am always trying to get the best "bang for my buck," I've crunched all the numbers and my chosen points system is the one that is the longest running. It is called cash. I can use it to buy luggage, or gift certificates, or travel on any airline, and my wallet is free of any cards of any kind. It can be used everywhere and I can even save the tax or get a better price at some places.

I have tried both cards and cash and I have found that using cash for everyday spending saves money. I recently tried to redeem two different points systems to get a trip to L.A. A ticket that would have cost me $371, including tax, to buy with cash would have taken $45,000 worth of spending with one credit card and $25,000 with another card. On top of that they would have charged $187 or $114.80 respectively for taxes and extra charges.

I really do not see how these point programs add up. Here is my logic. Using cash saves people up to 20% compared to using cards. You simply spend less money when you have to actually plop it down on the counter. Using cash puts a ceiling on your spending. If your spending virtue is in question—if you are being naughty with your money—using only cash is very helpful. The average yearly fee for points credit cards is around $120 a year. To build the points to fly to L.A. it would take me 2 or 3 years to charge $25,000 on my card, plus 2 or 3 years of fees. Remember, the flight only costs $371. Yikes!

Using a money clip is elegant and enlightened. Seriously. Look through your wallet and see all the tacky crap the retailers get us to carry around. If they weren't making money off the card, they wouldn't offer them, so we are paying extra to use them. Cash really is king. It keeps a ceiling on my spending, simplifies and streamlines my wallet, and gets me a better price on many things. Now that is a points system I can love!

However, there are free rewards cards and you can get them working for you. If you spend $100 a month on cable and $50 in cell phone bills, plus an average of $150 in work expenses a month, at an average cash back rate of 1% you would get $36 back a year. If you get travel points you can get a free flight every few years on these fixed expenses. Get a $0 card with great rewards. There are sites like *creditcards.com* that help you compare credit card benefits. Who said there is no such thing as a free lunch?

USE YOUR CREDIT WISELY

That said about the evils of credit cards, for your credit score ranking you need to show that you can borrow and pay off credit balances over a long period of time. Like fine wine, the best credit scores have been aged to perfection. Use only one credit card. Have all three of the large cards, and charge either work expenses or your fixed cell or cable bills every month to that card. Then have your bank set up an automatic payment so that at the end of the month you have the card completely paid off. This will make sure that you do not forget about the charges and let them build up and it will keep your credit score high when you need to borrow money.

GETTING THE BEST RATE

If you are a good client you should call your credit card company once a year to ask if the interest rate can be reduced. Tell them that you are looking at the interest rates of other companies and that you want the same rate. They should lower your rate. Try this for your cell phone bill too. Every year call the cell phone company and remind them that you have been a good customer for X number of years and you want a better rate or free voicemail.

I learned from my dad that you could always get what you want by being polite. He always gets what he wants, while at the same time the clerk feels good about the interaction. I followed his example when I had a shockingly high cell phone bill. I had gone over my minutes by an incredible amount, even though I had called the month before to ask for a plan that would limit me to $60 a month! I never like to pay more than $60 a month for my cell, which I also use as my home line to keep my costs low. When I called, I explained the situation and joked with the young woman, teasing her that I knew other carriers were coming out with the same new smartphone and I would change carriers just to be spiteful about my bill. I kept reminding her how shocked I was to see the bill. After going back and forth playfully for a few times and unleashing the full power of my charm (she *didn't* stand a chance), I had all of the extra minutes rolled back and I got a new plan that would limit me to $60 a month based on my data and calling patterns. Honey gets you a better cell phone bill than vinegar.

Honey gets you a better cell phone bill than vinegar.

Whenever I get a courtesy call from my cell phone company I ask what else I can get as an incentive to stay. I now have free voicemail, unlimited weekend calling, free phone upgrades every few years, and unlimited calling after 5 pm. If you do not get any help from the first contact at the credit card or cell phone companies,

> **Always ask for the "loyalty" department. They have the real power.**

always ask for their "loyalty" department. They have the real power.

Another time to get free stuff from customer service departments is when you have received bad service from them. Ask to talk to the manager to see how you can be compensated. I had a new credit card get delivered late and I almost got enough travel points for a flight to Montreal. The bigger the problem, the more free loot you should ask for.

DEPARTMENT STORE CARDS

Do not get department store cards. If you want to take advantage of your credit card's extended warranty program, or if you are buying on layaway and are nervous that the store could go bankrupt, always use one of the big three credit cards. Department store cards charge the highest interest rates by far and, as mentioned before, if you do not have the cash to buy something, do not buy it. Think of the buy-now-pay-later stores as casinos with ugly recliner sofas. They bet that most people who take the merchandise will not have the money to pay at the end of the year. They then charge up to 30% in interest. Pay in cash so you don't have to worry about having an emergency and end up without the cash to buy the product. Especially if the product is made of orange pleather.

6

INVESTMENT PORTFOLIOS

The biggest lie coming from Wall Street is that we cannot manage our investments ourselves. They have huge office towers with shiny wood desks, modern computers, and the best paid employees in the world. Who pays for the shiny towers, offices, wood desks, and outrageous salaries? You do. The fees you pay your broker, mutual fund manager, or financial planner contribute to the excesses of the financial sector. I have worked in finance and while I was there dealing with many high net worth individuals who were captains of industry, entrepreneurs, or from wealthy families, I always wondered, "Why would they take advice from someone making a fraction of their net worth?" They had built or managed these fortunes on their own. Why did they need a mutual fund manager? They didn't and neither do you.

When you discover how simple investing can be, you'll wonder why Wall Street exists at all.

Now I manage all of my investments myself. You can too. My strategies will save you up to 2-3% a year in fees. Over 20 years this will add up to quite a large sum of extra money for trips or cars or marble columns. When you discover how simple investing can be, you'll wonder why Wall Street exists at all.

OPEN A DISCOUNT BROKERAGE ACCOUNT

Brokers are at the mercy of the market and often do not see corrections or recessions coming, even though they work in the industry day in and day out. And yet many people are nervous about going out on their own and never open an investment account. It's when the market corrects and their savings get hit that they wonder why they didn't simply do it themselves and for less.

Open a discount brokerage account and save the management fees that can eat away at your savings. Mirror a favorite mutual fund or build a portfolio out of five diversified sectors that pay good dividends. You need to invest some time and do your own research for this strategy, but in the end it can save you money.

If you feel more comfortable with an advisor, by all means have one. An investment advisor can implement all of my strategies and you will still be able to get most of the cost savings. If your advisor gives you the sense that he or she is more of a sales person than a professional, show them the door. Your money must always come first.

ZERO EFFORT MILLION DOLLAR PORTFOLIO

This strategy is for people who cannot be bothered to invest more than 20 minutes on their portfolios, but who know that they have to invest for the future. I call it the "couch potato" fund. All you have to do is walk into a discount brokerage, set it up, and have the investments come off your paycheck each month. While these are index funds, the management fees are quite reasonable at .5%, and the lack of effort makes it worth it. In this example you will have $1.2 million in 30 years. Sound good? Here is what you do.

Google or look on *Morningstar.com* for the best dividend index fund. My favorite is the iShares Dow Jones International Select

Dividend Index Fund and the S&P Preferred Index Fund. The index funds invest in high yielding dividend or preferred stocks that pay out a stream of income to all of the unit holders. This strategy is normally meant for retirees and held outside of their retirement account in order to generate more income, but you can also hold it in your individual retirement plan, which is set up at your brokerage. (In Chapter 7, I discuss whether an individual retirement account is right for everyone, so be sure to read on.)

Currently these index funds pay per month or quarter. If someone were to invest $100,000 at today's 8% combined yield, the fund would pay out $8,000 annually.

Payout on Dividend Index Fund
$$\$100,000 \div 8\% = \$8,000/\text{year}$$

To make you the million with zero effort we are going to buy the first $5,000 (if you're under 50 years old at the end of 2010) or $6,000 (if you're 50 or older before 2011) inside your individual retirement account (IRA). Once your IRA is topped up, the rest can be bought outside of it. In this example, we will set up an $800 monthly automatic withdrawal program. Each month $800 comes off your pay and buys into the two funds. Set up the fund so that the distributions are reinvested to buy you more shares each month. As mentioned, in this example the fund pays 8%, so in your first quarter you will buy more shares with the distributions. The following quarter you will buy more shares with the reinvested distribution. Basically you will be getting almost a whole share free each quarter from the distributions. By the end of the year you will have ten free shares that will pay you 8% a year in dividends. You can see how it accelerates your savings.

Due to the nature of the two index funds, keep a balance of 50% U.S. Preferred and 50% International Dividend Income. Due to the high percentage of high yield blue chip stocks within the index, when the market goes south the diversification works as a natural hedge to buoy the funds. Dividend paying stocks perform better during downturns. Investors search for yield and short dollars have to pay the dividend if they short dividend paying stocks. Therefore they try to avoid it. By investing $800 monthly in this fund and reinvesting the monthly income, over 30 years the fund will grow to $1.2 million at a conservative 7.5%. The distributions will buy shares each month or quarter in good times and bad times lowering your average cost and increasing your yield. When you retire you simply tell the brokerage to pay the distribution out into your checking account instead of buying more shares. There—you have your own personal pension that took you 20 minutes to set up!

The extra benefit to this plan is that by placing $5,000 or $6,000 a year into your individual retirement account (IRA) each year you will also be getting a tax rebate of $1,500 if you are in the 30% tax bracket. That is a pretty good vacation fund every year for 30 years until you slip into your cozy 1.2-million-dollar retirement fund. The benefits to this plan go on and on: free vacation fund, retirement stability, and it is automatic. If you have more funds to invest or want to be more active with your investments, I will show you how to build your own income fund that operates under the same principles.

INDEX FUND PORTFOLIO

This is a portfolio for people with at least $40k to invest. Do not buy mutual funds; buy index funds. First, 80% of mutual funds do not outperform the market! Second, index funds are cheaper. You pay 1% or less as a management fee. Over many years the 2-3% management fee adds up to a huge amount. If your mutual fund only makes 2% per year and you pay a 2% management fee, you make $0. Had you invested in an index fund that also makes 2% and your index fund charges a 1% fee, then you make 1%. Why pay a management fee if the managers cannot beat the index?

When you choose an index fund you pay the real time free market to manage your investments. The market manages better than most mutual fund managers, who are under constant pressure from their superiors to perform. The way index funds work is they mirror a chosen market, such as the NASDAQ, New York, or other world indexes. Index funds can

> *Why pay a management fee if the managers cannot beat the index?*

also mirror industry sectors, such as REITs, royalty trusts, energy, or finance. Index funds rebalance themselves automatically based on the companies that make up the index.

In the late 1990s, when the tech boom was in full force, the top of the index was full of tech companies. As investors pushed up the tech stock prices they became dominant in the top 60 companies on the TSX (Toronto Stock Exchange). When the tech bubble burst and companies like Nortel collapsed, they dropped out of the TSX list of 60 top companies. In late 2008, agriculture stocks were the investment of choice. The market pushes up the popular stocks into the top holdings of the index and pushes out the less preferred ones in a much more cost-efficient way than managed funds. As long as the index continues to climb higher, so will your portfolio.

The best way to get around market risk is through diversification and dollar cost averaging. Choose four or five different index sectors and invest in them over the long run. One of the sectors should be an international fund. Use the powerful tactic of automatic monthly withdrawals to buy when the market is going up and going down. This will help you average down the cost of units and allow you to benefit when the market goes up again. This is called dollar cost averaging. Having these investment savings come automatically out of your account on pay day and buying a diversified set of index funds will set your retirement and savings on smart autopilot. Check with your broker or bank to see if they offer the feature. Knowing that you are doing the right things to ensure a solid retirement will give you many nights of good sleep and a feeling of control and confidence.

Here is an example of an index portfolio that is income oriented and made up of iShares index funds. This example has around a 6% yield that would be reinvested. Any growth on top of that would be gravy.

Index Fund Portfolio
25% DVY – iShares U.S. Dividend Index Fund
25% PFF – iShares U.S. Preferred Stock Index Fund
25% IDV – iShares International Dividend Index Fund
25% LQD – iShares Corporate Bond Fund

Making Your Own Index Portfolio

When you get enough money to start building your own portfolio you will be able to beat the performance of the index while at the same time providing yourself with a healthy income from your investments. Over the long run, investments that pay a dividend back to investors have not dropped as far in value in bad markets and have grown consistently when the market is moving upwards. When the market is down, you still receive the dividend, which helps cushion losses due to the downturn in the economy, paying you while you wait for it to turn around.

Warren Buffet is one of the most successful investors in the world. If you look at the type of investments Buffet buys, you will see that he purchases solid companies that pay good dividends. He owns shares in companies like Coca Cola, GE, Kraft, etc. These are all companies that will be around for the next 100 years. If you invest in companies that meet this criterion you can create your own index fund of solid, dividend-paying stocks that should be around for the long haul.

Mirroring index funds is how I build my portfolio and avoid the management fees. For example, I want to build an energy position within my account. I would buy the top ten holdings of the SPDR XLE exchange traded fund. Because it is hard to know which stocks will perform better than others, I prefer to buy the top ten stocks in the fund. That way you know that if the index goes up you will be profiting.

Here is an example of an Energy Index Portfolio. It will cost you $70 to set up at $7 a trade. If you purchase the SPDR XLE Energy Portfolio, they will collect and payout the dividends on their quarterly schedule. A benefit of holding the energy stocks in your own account is that you will be collecting the dividends in your own account as soon as they are paid out. If you purchased a $60,000 portfolio of the top ten energy stocks you would be saving $330 at .55% in management fees per year. The ten holdings listed below make up over 78% of the XLE Energy Index Fund. When the energy index goes up the top ten holdings will be the titans that lead. If dividends are decreased due to lower oil prices, these blue chips should be the last to cut dividends. Win, win on all fronts.

XLE Energy SPDR Top Ten Holdings

APC	Anadarko	$6,000
APA	Apache	$6,000
CUX	Chevron	$6,000
COP	Conoco Phillips	$6,000
DUN	Druon Energy	$6,000
XOM	Exxon Mobil	$6,000
HAL	Halliburton	$6,000
OXY	Occidental	$6,000
SLB	Schlumberger	$6,000
XTO	XTO	$6,000
Total Portfolio		**$60,000**

When the energy index goes up the top ten holdings will be the titans that lead.

BUILDING A PORTFOLIO FOR THE NEW ECONOMY

I believe that this new economic cycle will be a time of slower growth. Slower growth will limit the capital appreciation of many stocks. To compensate for this, slower growth investors should be looking for strong companies that return a solid 3% dividend, or more. When times get tough, people build positions in large dividend paying stocks and therefore there will be more of a demand for them. If there is not any growth in the stock price moving forward, investors hope to get a high dividend.

Many dividend-producing stocks are our most established companies. High yielding sectors are financial, telecom, energy, pharmaceuticals, and consumer goods. When you pick several great companies from each of these sectors you will be able to build a portfolio where you can always count on the dividends and diversification. Over time these quality companies have continuously increased their distributions helping your portfolio grow.

What I do is very simple. Knowing that over 80% of professional managers underperform the market and all of the fund managers use the index as a benchmark, why not let the market do the heavy lifting? Find an index fund that you would like to emulate. You can pick a U.S. or Canadian top dividend index fund or any other sector or market that you believe in. To work through an example I have chosen the XIU which is the S&P TSX LargeCap 60 ETF (exchange traded funds) from iShares. Canada hasn't been hit as hard in the global recession. It has a huge oil reserve and its banking system proved to be resilient. On iShare's website they list the top 60 companies on the index with their ticker symbols. It also shows you the breakdown of sectors like financials, energy, materials, industrials, telecom, etc., as per the chart below (S&P TSX Sector Breakdown). All are industries that pay high dividends and have demand moving forward.

S&P TSX Sector Breakdown

33.6%	Financials
27.3%	Energy
16.6%	Materials
5.03%	Industrials
4.99%	Telecommunication Services
4.30%	Information Technology
3.82%	Consumer Discretionary
2.46%	Consumer Staples
0.92%	Utilities
0.26%	Health Care

Take your total investment and break it up by the above percentages. So, if you have $100,000 to be invested you would have $34,000 for financials, $27,000 for energy, $17,000 for materials, etc. You do not need to have every small sector. For example, material stocks do not pay high dividends and therefore I only have one material company. This might sound unorthodox but tech, materials, and other sectors have been bid up by speculation and then bid right back down again. Having a solid dividend helps me weed these types of volatile sectors out of my portfolio. I am not in the mood for a short-term roller coaster ride.

Professional fund managers use the S&P TSX LargeCap 60 as a benchmark and therefore it will give you a sector breakdown when building your own index fund. To build your own portfolio you need to decode which stocks to buy in your chosen sectors. If you search online for the S&P TSX 60 holdings, you will find the stock weightings and ticker symbols as per the table (see S&P TSX LargeCap 60 Holdings) so that you can build each sector position. Most, if not all, of these stocks trade as ADRs on the New York exchange. We can buy them in $US and collect the dividends, eliminating any currency risk.

S&P TSX LargCap 60 Holdings

ROYAL BANK OF CANADA	RY	7.90%
TORONTO-DOMINION BANK	TD	5.94%
SUNCOR ENERGY INC	SU	5.75%
BANK OF NOVA SCOTIA	BNS	5.01%
ENCANA CORP	ECA	4.57%
RESEARCH IN MOTION	RIM	4.30%
MANULIFE FINANCIAL CORP	MFC	3.94%
CANADIAN NATURAL RESOURCES	CNQ	3.72%
BARRICK GOLD CORP	ABX	3.47%
POTASH CORP OF SASKATCHEWAN	POT	3.19%
BANK OF MONTREAL	BMO	3.02%
GOLDCORP INC	G	3.02%
CAN IMPERIAL BK OF COMMERCE	CM	2.78%
CANADIAN NATL RAILWAY CO	CNR	2.67%
TRANSCANADA CORP	TRP	2.31%
BCE INC	BCE	2.18%
SUN LIFE FINANCIAL INC	SLF	1.93%
TALISMAN ENERGY INC	TLM	1.92%
ROGERS COMMUNICATIONS—CL B	RCI.B	1.66%
ENBRIDGE INC	ENB	1.62%
KINROSS GOLD CORP	K	1.57%
CANADIAN OIL SANDS TRUST	COS.UN	1.49%
TECK RESOURCES LTD—CL B	TCK.B	1.43%
CAMECO CORP	CCO	1.30%
NEXEN INC	NXY	1.26%
BROOKFIELD ASSET MANAGE—CL A	BAM.A	1.16%
TELUS CORP	T	1.15%
IMPERIAL OIL LTD	IMO	1.09%
AGNICO-EAGLE MINES	AEM	1.03%
POWER CORP OF CANADA	POW	1.02%
SHOPPERS DRUG MART CORP	SC	1.00%

NATIONAL BANK OF CANADA	NA	0.99%
CANADIAN PACIFIC RAILWAY LTD	CP	0.94%
AGRIUM INC	AGU	0.88%
HUSKY ENERGY INC	HSE	0.81%
SNC-LAVALIN GROUP INC	SNC	0.78%
YAMANA GOLD INC	YRI	0.76%
THOMSON REUTERS CORP	TRI	0.71%
SHAW COMMUNICATIONS INC–B	SJR.B	0.65%
BOMBARDIER INC 'B'	BBD.B	0.64%
PENN WEST ENERGY TRUST	PWT.UN	0.64%
TIM HORTONS INC	THI	0.62%
FIRST QUANTUM MINERALS LTD	FM	0.61%
MAGNA INTERNATIONAL INC–CL A	MG.A	0.59%
CANADIAN TIRE CORP–CL A	CTC.A	0.49%
ELDORADO GOLD CORPORATION	ELD	0.47%
TRANSALTA CORP	TA	0.46%
FORTIS INC	FTS	0.46%
ARC ENERGY TRUST–UNITS	AET.UN	0.43%
METRO INC–A	MRU.A	0.43%
SAPUTO INC	SAP	0.39%
ENERPLUS RESOURCES FUND	ERF.UN	0.39%
LOBLAW COMPANIES LTD	L	0.35%
GILDAN ACTIVEWEAR INC	GIL	0.30%
WESTON (GEORGE) LTD	WN	0.29%
YELLOW PAGES INCOME FUND	YLO.UN	0.28%
INMET MINING CORPORATION	IMN	0.22%
BIOVAIL CORPORATION	BVF	0.20%
GROUPE AEROPLAN INC	AER	0.19%
MDS INC	MDS	0.06%

Take each ticker to your online brokerage, or Yahoo or Google Finance, where you can get free quotes. Note the stocks with the highest dividend yield. The great thing about this process is we already know that these stocks are top Canadian blue chippers, and that if they are declaring a dividend they are fairly safe.

For each stock, determine its percentage within the index and calculate how much of each stock should be in your portfolio. In the previous $100,000 portfolio example we had allocated $34,000 to the financial sector as per the sector breakdown. Royal Bank of Canada (RY) has a huge 4% dividend right now so I want it in my high yielding portfolio. I look at the stock breakdown and RY makes up 8% of the index. Therefore, I would buy $8,000 worth of RY shares and would subtract the $8,000 from the $34,000 allocated to my financial sector position.

If you do not know to which sector a stock belongs, you can find it online at Yahoo Finance under "Company Profile." Then build the rest of the financial sector with more high yielding stocks. Feel free to eliminate a stock that does not yield high enough for you. I look for stocks with a 3% or higher yield. The Financial Sector Portfolio Breakdown chart shows the financial sector broken down for my $100,000 invested portfolio example.

Financial Sector Portfolio Breakdown

Stock	Dollar Amount	Yield
Royal Bank (RY)	$8,000	3.62
Toronto Dominion (TD)	$6,000	3.77
Bank of Nova (BNS)	$5,000	4.19
Manulife (MFC)	$4,000	2.53
Bank of Montreal (BMO)	$4,000	5.6
CIBC (CM)	$3,000	5.4
Sun Life (SLF)	$3,000	5.0
National Bank (NA)	$1,000	4.23
TOTAL	**$34,000**	**$1,404.80**

Do the same with the telecom, energy, utilities, etc., sectors. I have provided an outline on how to build a portfolio. Take the largest companies with the highest yields. Customize it to support your personal yield and risk tolerance. If a stock is yielding a higher percentage and you are convinced of their strong fundamentals, buy more shares to increase your overall yield.

Building large positions of these dividend yielding blue chip stocks will also give you sophisticated trading opportunities. You can create additional streams of income from writing "covered option calls" or implementing "option strangles." I'll show you how to do this in the next section.

I (HEART) OPTIONS!

Selling Covered Calls to Double Your Yield

Going back to my philosophy that the world economy is down and out for a while, what I do is build on my strategy for yield. If we reference my Financial Sector Portfolio Breakdown Example in the last section I was receiving a 4% yield in tax-preferred dividends, which is awesome in itself. As mentioned the stream of dividends are from the best financial companies and I know they are the largest because I took them from the index fund that naturally ranks them by their size.

Next I look to sell options on each of these positions to double my yield. I look for stocks that I don't think have much upside in the next 3-6 months and that have more than 100 shares. Option Contracts are only bought and sold in lots of 100. Make sure that if you have less than 500 shares of a certain stock, or five option contracts, that it makes sense collecting the premium minus commission. With that small an amount it might not make that much sense.

With options you have calls and puts. A Call Option is when you have the right but not the obligation to *buy* a certain stock at a determined price at a determined time. The person selling you that option would collect a premium, just like insurance companies do. They collect a premium and provide you insurance for a certain time period for a certain death penalty.

If you become the option seller you collect that premium and if the stock price is at or above the agreed price on the determined date, the buyer takes the stocks.

Puts are the opposite of a Call. When you buy a Put you have the right but not the obligation to sell a stock at a certain price at a certain time. If you sell Puts as opposed to buying them you are offering to buy stocks at the price at which you issued your Put contracts and collected a premium for them.

Let's look at an example from my portfolio that I had built from the S&P TSX 60. I would take my largest positions where I didn't see much upside over the next few months and price out how much it would be to sell Calls. For example, say I owned 500 shares of the Royal Bank of Canada (RY) and I didn't see much upside.

RY NYSE – Royal Bank of Canada   500 Shares

I would price out how much it would be to sell five contracts of each in 3-9 months. Check your one-year chart to identify the chart resistance points and price the option premiums just outside that point. RY has traded up to $62.33 and as low as $44.51. I've checked in Yahoo Finance and the yearly target is $58.

What I then do is price the $60 Call January 2011 premium price. I've attached a chart of the RY Call Option premiums below. You can see the "Strike" price at $60 in the first column has a "Bid" price (how much I would receive per share when I sold Call Options on my already owned shares) at $0.65. That means that I would receive $0.65 × 500 shares which equals $325.

View by Expiration: Aug 10 | Sep 10 | Oct 10 | Jan 11

CALL OPTIONS: Expire at close Friday, January 21, 2011

Strike	Symbol	Last	Chg	Bid	Ask	Vol	Open Int
30.00	RY110122C00030000	18.00	0.00	21.60	22.60	10	14
40.00	RY110122C00040000	13.30	0.00	12.00	13.00	5	26
45.00	RY110122C00045000	9.30	0.00	8.00	8.40	4	532
50.00	RY110122C00050000	5.20	0.00	4.50	4.70	2	1,208
55.00	RY110122C00055000	2.25	0.00	2.00	2.20	5	2,044
60.00	RY110122C00060000	0.90	0.00	0.65	0.80	25	2,099
65.00	RY110122C00065000	0.25	0.00	0.10	0.25	25	361
70.00	RY110122C00070000	0.10	0.00	N/A	0.15	54	212
75.00	RY110122C00075000	0.09	0.00	N/A	0.15	0	121
80.00	RY110122C00080000	0.13	0.00	N/A	0.15	10	103

The scenario can go two ways for me here. If on January 21, 2011, when the option contract expires, RY is $60 or higher, I would lose my 500 shares but keep the profit having bought the shares at $50 plus my $325 option premium plus any dividends that I would be collecting during that time. If on January 21, 2011, the share price of RY is lower than $60, I would keep my shares, option premium and dividends too. I am obviously shooting for the stocks not to hit $60 so I get to keep everything, but if the stock does rise above $60 and I get my shares called or taken away from me, I simply re-buy the shares and sell the July 2011 contracts at a higher price again. My downside isn't much of a downside and the upside is huge for me!

Buying the shares at $50 would give me a cost base of $25,000 before trading costs. If each option contract was $0.65 × 500 that would give me $325 in premiums that I would collect the moment I sold the options.

$$\$0.65 \times 500 = \$325$$
$$\$325/\$25,000 = 1.3\%.$$

I would sell the calls in January 2011 and then again in June 2011 netting approximately the same amount of premiums. I would then be collecting an additional yield of 2.6% a year on top of my current RY dividend of around 4%. I have just now increased my yearly yield for my RY stocks from 4% to 6.6%! If I can do this for all of my appropriate stock holdings that will be an amazing extra source of income!

Option premiums are taxed as capital gains so it is extra lovable compared to regular bond income too. Extra love for options premiums. They paid my way through school and provide for an amazing life now. I heart options!

BUILDING YOUR POSITIONS BY SELLING PUTS

Whenever I build my positions, I always use Puts to do so. It is a way to get the market to pay me to by my position. Another way I've turned the market to serve me. Change your attitude towards money and win.

Now back to selling Puts. When you sell a Put as described above you have bought, for a premium, the right for someone to sell you stocks at a determined price on a determined time. Now you only acquire the stocks if the price of the stock is at or lower than the price you determined. Let's look at an example.

Example One: Just buying RBC (RY-N) shares. I would run out and buy them at the market price and pay my commission. Right now they are trading at $51.26 and I would buy 500 shares plus commission.

Buy 500 RY-N shares × $51.26 = $25,630 + $7 trading fee

Now if I think that in 3 months RBC will be slightly lower than $50 I could still buy them but collect a premium and lock in a lower price. I can sell Puts for five contracts (remember that options are in lots of 100) and collect $2.95 per contract for a total of $1,175! In 3 months I'll wait to see where the stock price is. You can sell Puts for one or any number of months out but I find that three has the best premiums versus time to acquire the stock.

Sell 5 Put contracts (100) × 2.95 = $1,475

If the market goes lower and by the third Friday of the month the RY-N share price is at $50 or lower than for what I sold the contracts, I would keep my $1,475 plus take possession of 500 RY shares at $50. If the shares were $50.01 or higher, the contract would expire as worthless, and I would still keep my $1,475 in premiums. Not too bad right?

I just collected 6% before I even got my shares. If the shares go down and I had just bought the stock they would have gone down anyway. If they go up and I get to keep the premium, I'll try to fish for them three months out again. I just keep trying for them until I get them. Now the downside to this is if RY-N rockets up and up and up and you can never acquire the shares, you would have missed out on all of that upside and missed the boat, right? In my experience it is very unlikely for dividend paying blue chippers to rocket like that. The fact that they have high dividends in the first place shows that they are not generally growth stocks. Plus, each time you missed obtaining the shares you collected that 6% premium. Not much of a miss in my opinion but try to use the strategy on stocks/industries that aren't likely to rocket.

If you do this for your entire portfolio you could generate a solid 3-6% before you even obtain the stocks. Why not get the market to pay you a premium and cover your commissions when building a portfolio?

I heart options!

Creating a portfolio that is diversified and paying solid dividends will ensure a retirement asset to fulfill your goals and aspirations. But retirement may be a long way off and you may have some goals to accomplish today.

WEALTH EQUALS
INCOME STREAMS

When people think of wealth they often think of having millions of dollars in the bank. However, when people who do not have a lot of money receive millions of dollars through the lottery or an inheritance they seem to burn right through it. Lotteries would be better if they paid the winner a large salary for the rest of their life! Then they could only spend what they got paid each month. True wealth is not only having loads of assets, but having the income streams that can come from assets. My philosophy of wealth is to make sure that every asset I have pays me the highest level of income it can.

My philosophy of wealth: ensure every asset I have pays me the highest level of income it can.

The common line from financial gurus is if you invest your money in an individual retirement savings account, that money is invested into the market and over time it will grow and you will have a solid asset for retirement. We have all heard the line that if we invest $800 a month for 30 years at 8% growth we will have 1.2 million bucks and be wealthy! Well, what if I cannot get that 8% growth? The last 8 years of growth were based on really cheap borrowed money. If that party is over, how can I expect the market to keep growing at an average of 8%? I cannot. But what I can count on is an investment strategy that pays me an income. That way I can count on that income if the market does not keep going up. Extra streams of income will also improve your lifestyle now, so you do not need to wait for retirement.

SUPPLEMENTING YOUR INCOME

Think about how you can supplement your salary with more streams of income. Even if you are happy with your job, more income can help to increase your retirement nest egg. Additional income can be banked and then used to invest in other income producing products until you are ready to depend on them entirely. This is how the wealthy get wealthier.

There are many investment strategies that can produce additional income. One is to buy monthly income or dividend funds or exchange traded funds (ETFs). Investment properties are another smart stream of income that can pay your mortgage and free up cash flow. By converting your basement into a rental apartment you can get your renter to help pay your mortgage. Think about buying a triplex so you can rent two of the apartments and live in the third one. Work the numbers to see if you can live for free and build equity by paying down the mortgage.

If you have a cottage, rent it for one of the three months in the summer to pay for the property taxes, repairs, or the purchase of a new deck. If you have an extra garage or parking space you will be amazed how much extra cash you can get by renting them. Little jobs on the side can really help too. I am an extra on TV shows when I have free time. A day sitting backstage, drinking coffee pays for my cell phone bill. Or better yet, a night of martinis.

I am sure there are lots of ways that you can increase your total income. Something you do in your spare time can become a business, for example developing websites, walking dogs, styling clothes or hair, consulting, writing creative copy, etc. Wealth really comes from multiple streams of income.

Start Your Own Business

Ask yourself what it is that you love to do? What are you really good at? What do you do for fun or as a hobby, and how could it be morphed into a profitable business? What could you do to make money that feels more like play than work?

Wealth really comes from multiple streams of income.

Once you have figured out what it is that you can do, market your services through Facebook or Craig's List, and see how much business you can generate. Any expense that you accrue can be deducted from your revenue, including computers, office space in your home, car expenses, etc.

To keep track of your business expenses, use a single credit card or bank account set up solely for business expenses. Then you will be organized for tax time. If you do incur any banking fees or card fees, they can be deducted as well. You will also be able to pay family members as employees to keep money in the family. The fringe benefits the company may be able to pay for country club memberships, luxury business trips, and company cars. You may even take loans out from the business.

Benefits of Incorporating

There are huge benefits for incorporating your own business. Any business expense can be deducted, just like when you were a sole proprietor, but corporations have lower tax rates than individuals. Also, you can pay yourself three different ways: dividends, salary, or loan. The most common payment option for incorporated companies is dividends. I explain my steamy passion for dividends later in this chapter. If you can pay yourself in dividends as an incorporated company you should.

Other benefits to incorporating are that you become a separate legal entity. A corporation has the same rights and obligations under U.S. law as a citizen. When a business is incorporated it develops a separate legal status from its shareholders and directors. Corporations can go into debt, acquire assets, enter into legal contracts, sue and be sued, and even be found guilty of committing crimes.

Limited liability is a benefit for the shareholders of a corporation. This means that the shareholders are not responsible for the corporation's debts. Creditors can't sue shareholders for debts incurred by the corporation. Therefore, incorporation is a way to protect your personal wealth.

Being a corporation will also give you better access to capital than a sole proprietor. The corporation has the option to issue bonds or share certificates to investors or other businesses. It provides more tools for expansion compared to other forms of business.

Finally, corporations last forever. A sole proprietorship dies when the owner dies, but a corporation lasts until it is dissolved. This makes transferring ownership easier to control.

RETHINKING INDIVIDUAL RETIREMENT ACCOUNTS

Whenever a talking head blindly tells you to put money into an individual retirement account, you should be skeptical. It might not be right for you.

There are many advantages to individual retirement accounts, like tax protection and tax returns. If you are in a secure job, in a high tax bracket, and you don't need your savings until retirement, then individual retirement accounts are great.

I prefer to have my money available to me. I have long-term goals of living in other countries and starting new endeavors, so it is more important for me to have my cash available. Here are three reasons why individual retirement accounts are not good for me and might not be good for you.

First, the money is stuck in my individual retirement account until I retire after age 59½. If there is ever a time when I need the money, I would not be able to access it without paying a penalty. I do not want to wait until I retire to enjoy it. What if there is a great investment opportunity in real estate, a special someone that I want to fly across the world with, or a chance to yacht around the Mediterranean? Sometimes a man has got to yacht!

What if there is a great investment opportunity, a special someone, or a chance to yacht?

Second, the money can only be used to invest in investment products like mutual funds, stocks, ETFs, or bonds. If a better investment vehicle ever showed itself, I would not be able to take advantage of it. Individual retirement accounts limit your options.

Third, when your individual retirement accounts turn into an income fund at 59½, it starts paying you distributions that are taxed as income—the worst type of taxation. If you had a dividend portfolio outside of your IRA or 401(K), the dividends would be tax preferred.

Last, I want to be able to leverage assets. I cannot borrow from an individual retirement account or lend against it to increase my profits or streams of income. It would be like a princess locked away in the tower who can only let her hair down when she turns 59½. That is a long time to wait for an asset.

DIVIDENDS ARE THE KEY TO MY HEART

Dividend payments are tax preferred in the U.S. when you buy American exchange traded stocks. If you have a bond that pays you $1 it is added to your income and taxed at the appropriate rate. If you get $1 of dividend income, it is now taxed at a maximum of 15% for most Americans. See my Dividend Versus Interest Income chart for a comparison. I give a whoop whoop to dividends.

Dividends Versus Interest Income

$100 Dividend Income	$100 Interest Income
$85 Income Kept	$65 Income Kept
$15 Tax Paid	$35 Tax Paid

Dividend Re-investment Plan (DRP) Programs

When you invest in dividend-producing stocks and you do not need the money for a while, ask your brokerage to set up a Dividend Re-investment Plan (DRP). As your dividends are paid out, they will buy more shares of the stock. Every quarter or month, when you collect your dividend payments, they purchase more shares. There is no trading cost for this service, so you continue to grow your number of shares for free!

Many of the blue chip stocks have discounted DRP programs too. This means that if you sign up for the DRP program, you get a discount on the reinvested dividends. For every share you buy with the DRP program you get a 2-5% discount below market value. Hello! Free shares at a discount! Here are some of the best blue chip dividend deals that you can find at *sharebuilder.com*.

- Bank of Montreal: up to 5% discount
- Bank of Nova Scotia: 2% discount

- Canadian Imperial Bank of Commerce: 3% discount
- Enbridge: 2% discount
- TransCanada Pipeline: 3% discount
- Telus: 3% discount

Research Your Dividend Stocks

When buying your stocks use these rules.

1. *Make sure you understand the business.* JP Morgan, Verizon, and Proctor & Gamble are all companies that I know and can see people using 100 years from now.

2. *In today's market, credit is hard to get because of the credit crisis.* Make sure that companies do not have much exposure on their balance sheet. In Yahoo or Google Finance you can search a company's liabilities, and then compare that level to their peers. If you are comparing banks, find out the average ratio of assets to debt.

3. *Compare the stock price to earnings ratios.* You can find this on your online broker's quote page. If they are within range of their competition, you will not over pay. Like shopping, I like to get stocks on sale, but I look more closely at the dividend yield and listen to their earnings report to hear if the dividends are ever in jeopardy of being cut and that their forecast is moving forward. You'll find this information on the "Investor Relations" section of each company's website.

4. *Remember that time in the market is more important than timing the market.* You have a 30% chance that your investment will go down in a year, but only a 1% chance of losing money in 30 years.

5. *Check out what the analysts and rating agencies have to say.* This is a good way to find out what the experts expect from the stock. You will be able to find this information under the "Research" area on your discount brokerage's website, or look for stock ratings on Yahoo or Google Finance. You want to see that your stocks have strong long-term growth potential to pay out the dividend.

6. *Keep away from "high flying" stocks.* Nortel never recovered after it was the tech star during the boom.

7. *Watch out for dividends over 10%.* This can mean that the stock has been beaten down for some reason and could cut its dividend soon. Do as much homework on the stock as possible to make sure that there won't be a dividend cut in the near future.

Respect your money. Don't follow standard advice and automatically plop it into an individual retirement account. Investigate other sources of income. Use dividends to offset taxes and keep more of your money. This way your money will respect you right back.

MORTGAGES AND INVESTMENT LOANS

Always do your research when borrowing money, whether for a home, a car, or to make an investment. Check out rates and options and make it work for you and your money.

MORTGAGES—A SPECIAL KIND OF LOAN

A home is usually the biggest investment we make in our lives. It is virtually tax free when you sell it, and you can get the best interest rates from mortgages. On top of that, you can write off your mortgage interest too. When shopping for a mortgage, be sure to look around online, find the best rate, and take it to your bank for them to match or beat. If you have several other products with the same bank, such as car loans or bank accounts, you deserve their best rate so be sure to ask for it.

Banks make a huge amount of money through mortgages. If you have a $200,000 mortgage at 6% interest, paid semi-monthly for 25 years, you will actually pay $383,411 in total. That's close to twice the amount of the mortgage!

Most people have their payments come out of their accounts once or twice a month. By setting up the payments to come out bi-weekly you will be making slightly lower payments every two weeks, which means two extra payments per year. Those two extra payments end up saving you thousands over the term of the mortgage. The faster you pay off the mortgage, the more you save.

The second "quick win" when paying off the mortgage faster is to round up your payments. See the difference in the rounding up example. Who would have known that an extra $61 paid bi-weekly would save you an additional $18,542 in interest over the term of the mortgage?

Rounding Up on a $200,000 Mortgage

Amortization	Payment	Interest Paid	Payment
25 yrs	Semi-Monthly (24)	$183,411	$639
18 yrs	Bi-Weekly (26)	$122,854	$700

Variable vs. Fixed Rates

This is really a market-timing question. Statistics show that over time you do better with a variable rate. However, if you are applying for a mortgage when the lending rate has been reduced severely, you can assume that it will eventually go back up, so it makes sense to get a fixed rate. If a variable rate makes you nervous due to the chance that it will go up, then a fixed rate to lock in your payments for the term is the way to go. If you are considering selling in the short term, then an open variable rate is the only rate that will leave the mortgage open for you to do so.

Paying Property Taxes

Do not let the bank pay your property taxes. They'll collect the interest on that money instead of you. If you pay $2,000 in yearly property taxes, set up an automatic withdrawal to place the money into your high interest savings account. If it pays 3% you will make $60 in interest in a year. Make sure you are always making the system work for you. Let the bank pay you instead of the reverse.

INVESTMENT LOANS

Here is my strategy for getting a free investment portfolio (which is working quite well for me at the moment). Go to the bank and get an investment loan.

As an example, let us say $60,000. You take the $60,000 and invest it. Investment loan interest rates vary but you should be able to get one for prime plus 0.5% or 1%, which would currently put it at 2.75-3.25%, for an open variable loan amortized over 15 years. The huge benefit of the investment loan, compared to a standard loan, is that you can deduct the loan's interest as an expense. You will also be paying a much lower interest rate compared to standard loans due to the fact that the loan is pledged against the investments.

> *Make sure you are always making the system work for you.*

The bank will secure the loan with the investments and you have two options for investing. The first and easiest is monthy index funds. Again, my favorite income funds are the iShares U.S. Preferred and the iShares iBoxx Invest Grade Corp Bond. The combined yield is around 6.5% and it distributes $325 per month. Since the monthly loan payments would be $421.60, you're almost completely covered.

The two funds' equal balance of 50% in bonds and cash and 50% in blue chip high-yield U.S. Preferred Shares provides a natural cushion for any market corrections. Through the worst part of the last correction the LQD iShares Investment Grade Corp. Bond Fund did not drop nearly as badly as the overall market. It is also reassuring that through the last 2 years of the economic downturn the two funds did not decrease their distributions. They have been consistent around $0.42 to $0.47 since 2004 or $0.18 to $0.25 for the preferred fund.

> *I love my money way too much to give up the management fee for the index funds.*

The second option is to create your own monthly income fund within your own account. I love my money way too much to give up the management fee for the index funds, so I have purchased the following portfolio on the TSX (Toronto Stock Exchange) to pay down my investment loan.

My Portfolio

Company	Index Symbol
Cineplex Galaxy	CGX.UN
Bell Alliant	BA.UN
Liquor Stores	LIQ.UN
Altagas Services	ALA.UN
Futuremed	FMD.UN
Activenergy	AEU.UN
Pengrowth Energy	PGF.UN
Paramount Energy	PMT.UN
Penn West Energy	PWT.UN
Canadian Oil Sands	COS.UN

I have purchased roughly $5,000 in each stock. They are diversified properly among many sectors and are all high yielders with upside potential in cases of market recovery or commodity price increases, such as oil. This basket of trusts generates $6,000 a year or $500 a month in income to cover the costs of the investment loan. All have appreciated in price as the market has risen and I expect the oil trusts to increase their distributions as oil prices continue to rise.

As you can see my portfolio is built of stocks that are Canadian income trusts denoted buy the ".UN" at the end of the symbol, as in "CGX.UN". This means they are stocks that pay out a high percentage of their earnings in income streams. I'm also sure all of the market followers out there are thinking, "The trusts convert back to regular stocks in 2011—what then?" Well, most income trusts are expected to convert to high yielding stocks, like Crescent Point (symbol "CPG" on the TSX) just has, and if one of my selections does not convert, I will swap it for one that has. That is exactly what I did to get a free portfolio! Plus, it increases over time as the underlying trusts increase in value. The New York Stock Exchange includes royalty trusts like BP Prudhoe Bay Royalty Trust (BPT), which has a 9% yield currently. You can build a similar portfolio with U.S. royalty trusts and REITs.

GET CREATIVE WITH LOANS

If you are creative with loans, they can sometimes help you achieve things that you could not have imagined were even possible. You just need to be resourceful. I purchased my first property with a demand loan.

I had just finished school and had $27,000 in student debt. I also had $10,000 that I had made in the market. I taught myself to trade options when I was in university. If I had spent as much time studying as I did trading options I may have been a Rhodes Scholar.

Normally someone with a negative net worth of $17,000 and an entry-level job would not qualify for a mortgage, but I was creative. I borrowed $20,000 and made interest-only payments. I then got a pre-approved mortgage and used my $10,000 of savings combined with $7,000 from the loan to put down a 10% deposit to buy a $165,900 condo.

I bought from plans when they were converting a 100-year-old factory into residential lofts in a part of town that was on its way up. A chic boutique hotel had just opened around the corner 2 years prior and the old rundown retail stores had started to turn into art galleries, which is the first sign that a neighborhood is turning around.

Once I put down the $17,000 deposit, I had 1.5 years until the condo would be built. I then advanced the remaining $13,000 of the loan into my individual retirement account and received $3,250 back in a tax return, which I added to my retirement account. I saved an additional $3,750 which brought me to the $20,000 that Canadians can take out of their retirement accounts to buy their first homes. In the U.S. you can take out $10,000 and save the 10% penalty.

When the $20,000 had been in my retirement account for the mandatory 3 months, I withdrew it and paid off the initial $20,000 loan 6 months before I moved into my new loft, saving myself some interest.

By the time my building incorporated and my mortgage started, I had made enough money to be approved on the mortgage. I essentially took a negative net worth and low income and made the best of the situation. Three years after I had bought my place it doubled in value and I had a very low mortgage.

Loans can work to your advantage if you use the system to benefit you; either with interest deductibility or by purchasing something like an appreciating real estate investment.

9
INSURANCE

Insurance is one of those things we love to hate, but we're so glad it's there when we need it. Something that you pay for when you're alive to benefit everyone but you when you die. The real trick is making sure you have enough insurance and the right kind.

HOW MUCH INSURANCE

Insurance can seem complicated but it is quite easy once you know a few rules.

Insurance— only get what you need.

Here is a quick rule to figure out how much insurance you need. Calculate how much of your income your family relies on and what you would need to replace it. Your insurance needs to pay off all your debts and replace your income with an estimated 5% return. Here is a quick example.

1. You make $60,000, so at 5% a year you would need $1.2 million to generate $60k per year.
2. You owe $200,000 on your mortgage.
3. You owe $10,000 on your car loan.

4. You need $50,000 for each of your children to go to university.

A quick calculation tells us you need $1,460,000. After your family has gone through the horrible stress of losing you, you want to make sure that their financial stresses are wiped out and that your income is covered. Knowing that your family is taken care of if something happens to you will give you peace of mind.

WHAT KIND OF INSURANCE

The only insurance to get is *term insurance.*

Get it early when you first have a family, and get it term to 100. This will guarantee your premium at a younger age and carry it through until you die or you turn 100. When you turn 100 you stop paying for insurance. (It is always nice to have things to look forward to.)

Universal insurance only benefits the sales people universally. Universal insurance programs build up an investment portfolio along with the insurance, which is much more expensive to operate than having the investment account by itself. Term insurance does not have an investment component, so it saves you a lot of money in management fees.

MORTGAGE INSURANCE

Mortgage insurance will pay only what you have left on your mortgage when you die. If you owe $1 on your mortgage when you die, the bank will pay that dollar and only that dollar. However, the premiums you pay for the insurance stay consistent until you pay that last dollar of the mortgage.

Term insurance is better than mortgage insurance because it does not decrease coverage over time and the premiums stay consistent over the term of the policy. If you get a $1 million policy for term 100, the payments will stay consistent and the $1 million will not decrease. Make sure that you have enough to pay off your mortgage in your term policy so mortgage insurance is not necessary.

DISABILITY

If you have a family, ask your insurance specialist if you need to top up any coverage you have from work. The human resources department at work will be able to tell you what your coverage is so you can decide if you need to top it up. Use the same equation above to figure out how much disability coverage you need to keep your standard of living if something happened to you and you could not work. Disability is crucial if you're self-employed and have a family.

SHOP AROUND

Be sure to shop around for insurance. My parents had been with their firm for millions of years. When I kept pushing them to shop around, they saved thousands. There are many discount insurance shops that are being very aggressive with their pricing. If you have home plus boat plus car insurance you will save plus, plus, plus! Do a search for the best rates online and then search for any affiliated groups with your work, alumni, or leisure groups. You'll be shocked at how much you'll save if you have an affiliation with a larger group.

Once they've given you the rate be sure to keep shopping it around. Call your original insurer and tell them that you're about to move unless they beat that rate. Keep searching until you get the best insurance for the cheapest rate.

10 SHOPPING

In the introduction I talked about how I like to shop. Instead of shopping "willy-nilly," shopping should be well planned, well executed, and examined afterwards. Shopping is like a battle.

EFFICIENT SHOPPING

The first thing I do is scout for the things I want to go on sale and keep a watch on them. I very rarely pay for anything that is not on sale. If there is something that I want that is not on sale, I keep checking back until it is. Learn when the semi-annual sales are, and when they get new inventory and the old inventory goes to the sale section. Whenever you are about to buy something always smile and ask if it is going on sale soon? Then come back later and snatch it up for less!

Once you see that something is on sale you need to play the inventory game. As inventory goes down, the price will go down. Wait while your size is plentiful to see if you can time the price reduction properly so that you get your size at the cheapest price possible. Then attack when the moment is right. Show no mercy! If an item never goes on sale, you probably don't really want it.

Shopping is all about quality, not quantity. Make sure that the things you buy make your heart go "thump." This will save you money in the long run and allow you to have a more uncluttered life. For instance, everything in your closet should make you feel like a million dollars when you wear it. Sweaters sitting at the back of the closet with the tags still on are wasted income that could have been invested.

> **Make sure that the things you buy make your heart go "thump."**

One of my clients has an amazing raincoat that she has had for 10 years now, and she wears it all the time because it is a classic, and she looks great in it. Over the 10 years she has spent nothing—zero—on other rain jackets. She has her "Platonic Form" of a jacket and, even though it was expensive, she loves it every time she wears it. She will continue to love it because it is great quality and will last forever. If you average the cost of the coat by the amount of wear she has gotten, she is way ahead of the game. Smart purchase, lady friend!

If I see something that I like but get the feeling that it is just an impulse buy, I wait 24 hours and then go back. If it still gives me butterflies, I buy it. Anything that I buy has to make me feel good, be something that I see myself getting a lot of use from, and be a "Platonic Form." Buy classic pieces that will last forever, and be stylish forever, so you will get that "wow" feeling every time you use it.

GROCERY SHOPPING

Grocery shopping is something I hate. I had only made a handful of grocery store visits by myself by the time I had reached my mid-20s. I could not get over how expensive everything was, so I preferred to just eat out and not have to worry about the dishes. Plus, I kept my extra shoes in the oven.

Now that I am older I have discovered the merits of grocery shopping. It is healthier to eat fresh products than to eat out all the time. I can also save money by eating at home so that once a week I can have a fancy meal out with friends.

I have grown to tolerate grocery shopping by challenging myself to re-create expensive frozen and processed foods for less money. For example, one jar of fancy tomato sauce in the store is around $5. I can buy tomatoes, garlic, hot sauce, and spices cheaper than that, while at the same time controlling the preservatives and salt content. Frozen pizza is the same. I can make a fresh pizza (with extra olives) for a fraction of the cost of a frozen pizza and all of my monetary and health savings work towards getting me closer to my personal goals. (I have found a new place for my extra shoes.)

Fill your fridge with fresh veggies, fruits, and nuts. Give the kids a veggie tray instead of chips or candy. Have a jug of filtered water with sliced lemons or limes (or cucumbers or strawberries) instead of pop or sugary juices. Water quenches your thirst and saves you money at the same time. When I stopped buying pop and chips I lost 10 pounds.

Shopping at farmer's markets is another way to support our farmers and get the freshest produce, while returning savings to other investments. The farmer's market is a nice change from stuffy grocery stores, and I am proud to buy locally, instead of buying food shipped in from around the world. Buying locally is better for the environment and better for your money.

ELECTRIFY YOUR SAVINGS!

Electricity conservation is very important for the environment and because our grid is under stress in parts of North America. I play a game to get my electricity bill as low as I possibly can. This fits nicely within my overarching philosophy of not wasting a single penny if it could be working harder for me in an investment or savings account. Sending money to the electricity company has never been on my goals list, believe it or not.

Here's a list of simple things to do to beat your last month's bill.

- Do not pre-heat the oven—just stick the food in—unless you are baking.
- Do not run more than one appliance at the same time.
- Try to only run appliances after 8 pm.
- Change all your old light bulbs to low energy CFL bulbs.
- Use timers for outside lights.
- Unplug chargers or appliances that you are not using.
- Turn off cable boxes and TVs—standby still takes energy.

> *Sending money to the electricity company has never been on my goals list!*

There are several local electricity distributor programs that will pick up old fridges or freezers in the basement, offer rebates for high efficiency furnaces, and programs that offer air conditioning units with an automatic power-off feature when the grid is under stress. Getting rid of an old fridge can save you up to $150 a year. All of these programs can save you money and help the environment in the meantime.

VACATION SHOPPING

I am well known for getting the trendiest boutique hotel, best five star on the beach, or first class ticket for pennies. Whenever I travel with friends they plop me in front of a computer and cheer as I get rooms, flights, and book amazing restaurants all for exceptionally low prices.

My trick is to first scout out the locations of the coolest hotels. I look for traditional five stars on the beach, historic hotels in the old part of town, or chic boutique hotels located around neat cafes, bars, shopping, and restaurants. Once I have my gem of a hotel that makes me shiver at the thought of staying there, I open six windows on my computer and start searching for "Cheap W Hotel," or whatever the name is. I'll follow each link and then type in the date I'm staying and click "continue" until I can see the complete price in the check out window. I'll also compare those prices to similar hotels that many of the discount hotel sites will offer up to you.

Once I have the *ultimate* hotel at the very best price I do one last thing. I Google for a promotion code for that hotel. There is normally a promotion code box. I'll try each code I find to bring the price down as low as I can. This works for rental cars too. If you search "hertz promo code" you'll find amazing hits on the web that'll get you company or association deals. I simply keep trying the codes until I know that I can't beat the price that I'm about to book. Then I close my notebook and bask in the glory of getting my ideal hotel for the cheapest price.

Airline tickets work the same way. I'll open six windows and Google "cheapest flight to Sydney" or wherever I'm going. For example, I'll look at short flights from Buffalo or Detroit on Jet Blue or American Eagle to L.A. and then on to Sydney, Australia, after that. On a long flight you can get a short haul to a major hub on a discount airline and then get a super cheap flight to the final destination. This little trick has literally saved me thousands of dollars on flights abroad. To go to Europe I'll fly to London, spend some time with friends there and enjoy the break in flight length. Then I'll get a Ryan Air or Easy Jet flight to my actual destination for a *huge* discount. I flew to Malta this way and saved over $1,000 on a direct flight. You can use the same strategy flying through Germany and Holland. I like to change it up so I can spend a day or two in a different European hub every time I visit my favorite continent.

Once you are at the airport, hang back a little and see how many people are getting on the flight. I always book coach but I wait until the last moment to check in. When I do I always wear a tie and jacket, then give my biggest smile and ask if there is room in business. It is amazing how many times this has worked. If the plane is full they will bump the last passengers to business. I once got a bump up to first class going all the way to Japan, which was simply bliss. I had lamb and champers all the way there and was able to stretch out and get an amazing sleep to awake all bright-eyed and bushy-tailed to meet my brother when he was working in Japan. The gods got back at me on the way back, however. The plane was full and I didn't get a business class ticket. Instead I got a seat that wouldn't recline, in front of the bathroom on a very long Pacific flight, beside a gentleman who took off his socks to reveal velociraptor-like toe nails that dug into the carpet. How I missed first class that flight. Over the long run I've travelled many flights in business class that I haven't paid a cent toward. I *heart* business class.

ALWAYS BUY LUXURY CARS

I love cars so this is advice that other car enthusiasts will enjoy. My love of cars started when I was very young. Before I could drive, I would get dad to drive me to the car dealerships so I could check them out. For my 16th birthday all I wanted was for someone to let me test drive my favorite car at the time. A BMW key chain was my most cherished Christmas gift one year. I kept if for years and years as the fob to my house keys. I also bought myself leather driving gloves with the knuckles cut out.

Whenever I travel in Europe I visit the great car manufacturers. When my brother and I were backpacking through Europe as students, I convinced the woman at BMW's headquarters to admit us on the tour of the 3 Series plant, even though the tour was full and neither of us spoke German.

But cars are expensive and they depreciate in the blink of an eye. So why not get the market to pay for expensive depreciating items? When a car drives off the lot it instantly loses up to 30% of its value! Buying a luxury car will provide you with better resale value and greater demand. If you look at the J.D. Power and Associates website for the best overall dependability, Lexus, Cadillac, Acura, BMW, and Jaguar are all in the top ten. Buy a luxury car that is 1-3 years old and keep it until it is 6 years old to get the most money out of it. You will get better features, a more luxurious car, and usually better safety—more bang for your buck. Plus, you get to drive a luxury car!

> **Remember that all companies make their money off the average "Joe," so never be "Joe."**

Once you've found your dream car and negotiated a good price for it, buy the car with cash. Remember also to ask if the dealer has affiliate pricing for partner companies. If you or your partner works for a large company you might be on the list of preferred companies and get an extra percentage off the price. Remember that all companies make their money off the average "Joe," so never be "Joe." Do whatever you can to get an insider discount.

Once you have the cash for the car and you have negotiated the best price (remember that cash always demands a better price), then go to your bank and ask for an investment loan for the same amount as the price of the car. If you take $30,000 out of your investments for the car, then put $30,000 back into your investments with an investment loan. It gives you the flexibility to sell the car when you want to, and it makes the interest on the loan tax deductible. Buy a portfolio of high yielding stocks like real estate trusts, banks, oil trusts, etc. Get stocks or high yielding ETFs (exchange traded funds) that pay monthly so as your investment loan comes out of your account it will be paid back with the income from the dividends.

You will have a $30,000 portfolio of monthly paying high yielding trusts that pay you around $250 a month at 10% a year and a $30,000 loan at 6% for 15 years that will cost you around $255 a month. If the market continues to go up over time like it has in the past, the portfolio's value will also appreciate. If your portfolio doubles faster than the 15-year amortization, you can pay off the loan faster.

Your risk here is that the companies could lower their dividends, but if you diversify and watch for them to cut dividends, you will still be further ahead than just paying full interest on the loan and watching the asset depreciate. Your increase in market price over the next 15 years, based on past market performance, should outpace the interest you pay each year, plus you have the payments covered each month except for $5. When you need a new car in 6 years you just up the loan, trade in your car, and do it all over again. The car versus investment loan chart shows you the benefit of the plan.

CAR LOAN VERSUS INVESTMENT LOAN

Option	Loan	Interest Per Year Paid	Additional Income	Investments Portfolio After 15 Years
Buy car with $30k loan	$30,000 @ 6% for 5 years = $580/ month	$5,000 in non-deductible interest	$0	$0
Buy car with cash, invest $30k	$30,000 @ 6% for 15 years = $255/month	$5,000 minus tax deduction = $3,500/year	$250/month to pay loan @ 10%	$30,000 plus growth based on market

Leasing is for Losers

Did you know that when you lease a car you pay the interest on the entire amount of the car, minus the down payment, even though you have to give it back at the end of the lease? It makes much more sense to buy a car that is 2-3 years old and take out a loan for up to 3 years. Your car insurance will be cheaper because it is an older car and you will not get into any mileage traps at the end of the lease. Always buy the car. If you cannot afford to finance it for up to 3 years, you cannot afford it.

GET THE MARKET TO PAY

Many of the energy royalty trusts are returning over 10% yield now that they have taken a tumble from their one-time highs. A great way to lessen the cost of oil at the pumps and food at the grocery store is to invest in oil and agriculture companies, and let them help pay for your gas and groceries. If you invest $5,000 in five different oil royalty trusts, at 10% you will earn $41.66 a month towards your fuel bill. Why not benefit from having to pay the higher prices? Permian Basin Royalty Trust (PBT) and Penn West Energy Trust (PWT) are great examples of this.

SELL EVERYTHING BEFORE YOU THROW IT OUT

My brother and I had been storing our childhood Star Wars, G.I. Joe, and Transformer collections in our parents' basement for the last 20 years. When we were bored one evening we set up every toy on the pool table and took pictures of them. Then we put them up for sale. We sold all three lots for over $1,000! Now that is real found money.

After our success with the toys, we sold our comics and collectibles. We took mom and dad out for a nice dinner to compensate them for 20 years of storage fees. When I was moving, anything that I didn't want I put up for sale on Craig's List, which paid for the moving van. What seems like junk to you may be valuable to someone else.

MONEY AND RELATIONSHIPS

Money is the one item that everyone dances around when dating. Let's throw it right into the middle of the date table and address it!

Have you noticed that the first two questions out of someone's mouth are "where do you live?" (translation: "What kind of real estate can you afford?") and "what do you do?" (translation: "How much money do you make?"). Being cognizant of this can help you not only pick a great mate but a great money person too.

If you find someone who truly loves their money and is in control of it, you can be confident that they are in control of their life. Someone doesn't necessarily need to make gobs of money but if they follow the next few rules it reflects positively on how they will manage their relationships.

1. *Money balance: Do they make more than they spend?*
   This shows you that they are confident and in control of their lives. They don't need to spend excessively to try to make themselves happy. They don't need to live a life-style above what they can afford to impress anyone. They

are self-assured. It also shows that since they can balance their cheque book, they'll have balance in other parts of their own lives.

2. *Savers: Do they have savings?* If your potential snookums has a "saver" mentality, as opposed to a "spender" mentality, that equates to a planner, a committer, and someone who will be a "Steady Ship" for the long haul.

3. *Asset lover: Assets equal commitment.* If your date loves big assets, like I do, then you are set. It shows that they can commit, that they're building a foundation. They are responsible and forward-looking. It also shows that they are looking to grow roots and nest at some point if the asset is something like a family home.

4. *Debtless: Do they only have positive debt?* Does your date have bad debt or emotional baggage? Many times people overspend because they are unhappy and they try to buy themselves some bliss. All of us can get caught up with trying to keep up with the "Joneses." Even though your date makes a lot of money they may spend it all too. This is a race that no one ever wins. Those Joneses are quick like bunnies! If your date isn't in the black, ask for the check and keep looking.

> **Money problems are never money problems; they are always people problems.**

Money problems are never money problems; they are always people problems. If you see someone who doesn't love their money, it could be a window to another problem. Make sure that everyone you date loves their money by being a balanced saver and an asset lover and save yourself some grief down the road.

SUMMON YOUR MONEY MATCH

Money is the number one reason that relationships blow up. You can eliminate that risk by picking someone who is compatible with you. One way to do this is to write down exactly what kind of characteristics your stock stud or dollar diva will have. Use Exercise 5 to create your perfect money match and then go out and find him or her.

EXERCISE 5

Your Perfect Money Match

On a piece of paper, describe how your perfect money match is with money. Consider these points:

How much do they make?

_____

_____

_____

_____

Are they frugal but not cheap?

_____

_____

_____

_____

Are they generous to the people they really love?

_____

_____

_____

_____

How do they spend their money and what value does it bring them?

_____

_____

_____

_____

What kind of ambitions do they have?

_____

_____

_____

_____

Describe them on paper to fit your vision of your perfect money match. Like a lighthouse, you'll beam this ideal out when dating and you'll quickly attract these types. You'll also instantly see if someone is not up to par.

Why waste years ignoring something that could be dealt with upfront? Money problems have hidden under the rug for too long. Life is so much better after addressing issues straight on, especially in relationships.

CREATING FINANCIAL ABUNDANCE
WITH YOUR LIFE PARTNER

Once you've picked a great partner make a deal with them to generate the feeling of abundance in all areas of your life together. Go through the Goals Exercise (Exercise 3) in Chapter 3 again with your partner. Create a plan for universal personal and financial wealth. Think how you want to spend your money on family, friends, charity, etc. Wealth isn't only how you're going to spend your money but also how you can spend your time. Decide on all the ways you both can create wealth for yourselves, financially and otherwise.

Sit down and discuss where you are financially and where you want to be, like in a business arrangement. The key here is to be honest with yourself and each other—you're a team now. How much do you have? How much do you owe? Write it down in black and white so you both know where every penny is spent and where your assets and debts lay. Keep your fingers holstered when you see who spends more. You'll need each other to get to where you want to go and getting stuck in the mud over who is to blame is no way to start.

Work out a budget. Decide upfront what can be cut in order to get you to your ideal future of abundance. Even if you and your partner are quite well off, decide how you can increase your income and decrease your expenses and then allocate the difference towards your goals as partners. The sense of well-being, wealth, and abundance will come when the list below is satisfied.

1. Money is free flowing to pay all of your bills and afford you your chosen lifestyle.

2. Love is given and received. Family, companionship, friendships are strong and all encompassing.

3. Retirement is well funded and you are confident that either pensions or streams of income from property or investment will cover your monthly costs until death.

4. Time is still on your side. You know that all of the things you want to achieve in life are still possible.

5. Health is present. Vitality still favors you and you have the ability to do and see everything that you choose.

FINANCIAL CHECKUPS

A financial check-up is needed every month. Take a look at all of your statements from your budget box and see how you are tracking. There are three main components to review.

1. *Review your investments.* Reinvest any dividends that you have collected into other investments that will also pay you dividends.

2. *Review your goals list for the year.* Savor what you have achieved and what you can look forward to in the coming months. This will give you a sense of accomplishment and motivate you to keep working towards your goals.

3. *Create your own balance sheets during your financial check-ups.* Write down all of your assets and then all of your liabilities. Calculate your net worth by subtracting your liabilities from your assets. I do this once a month to see how my savings and investment plans have increased my net worth month by month. You'll be motivated to save more by watching your net worth go up and up.

FINANCIAL COACH

A great way to figure out how to be good with money is to learn from people who are financially successful. Who are the wealthiest and happiest people you know? Ask if you can buy them dinner or coffee and take your savings and investment plan. See if they can add any value to your plans. If they have made money in a certain way or have had success financially, you might be able to learn from them. Have a few financial mentors and meet with them regularly to share your accomplishments or to bounce ideas off of them. Their life experiences will help you out when you are getting started.

Have a few financial mentors and meet with them regularly.

A Financial Coach will also assist you in unlocking your unlimited potential. They will inspire you to dream big and determine your core values. They will encourage you, help you to overcome your internal blocks, and encourage you to discover what you truly want from life. Coaching has become a powerful tool for executives and motivated individuals who want to push on to higher levels of achievement. A high percentage of Fortune 500 executives have executive coaches to keep their competitive edge high.

CONTINGENCY FUND

Everyone should keep 5-8 months of income in an emergency fund. Some people keep a stack of $100 bills in a safety deposit box. If you ever lose your job or get into an accident, or if a family member is in trouble, you will have the money. Your savings can also be used for emergencies provided that you pay back the fund when the crisis is over.

HOW WILL YOU KNOW WHEN YOU ARE SUCCESSFUL?

Be sure to spend some time thinking about how you will know when you have reached your "Platonic Life." Visualize in detail what it will look like. Many people race towards success without first defining it, so they never reach it. They have no way to know when they are successful. Write down how your ultimate life will work, including a day-to-day schedule.

When you are living this perfect life you will recognize it and know you have made it. It is very important to celebrate your successes, and then continue on towards new goals.

LOVE IT FOREVER

Some people believe that money is an end in itself, but it is really just the means to an end. Money can enable a better life. This is the real reason you should love your money.

I used to hate my job. I would pull the covers over my head in the morning because I did not want to go to work. I said horrible, horrible things to my teddy bear as I got showered and dressed. I was going through the motions of life, which is a terrible way to live. I wasn't satisfied by my accomplishments at work. I had a great salary but I wasn't getting any richer. I worked 8 am to 8 pm and then partied on weekends to de-stress. I knew that life had so much more to offer me, but I just hadn't tapped into it yet.

Finally I decided to figure out what I really wanted to do. I recognized what my strongest values were and then built my life around them. I spent time discovering what would make me the happiest (not just happy but the *happiest*) and then I went after it full force.

Within one year I could list a number of accomplishments and dreams fulfilled.

- I had started my own business that combined my passion for money and finance with my love of helping people live the very best lives that they can. I became financially independent by developing several streams of income and none are considered work for me. I trade my accounts, write about a subject I am interested in, and coach young executives to live their "Platonic reality."

- I spend much more time with my family—whether they like it or not. I have time to visit my grandpa and hear his great stories from the past. I have set weekly dinner nights with my parents and family. I either get a home-cooked meal or we try out a trendy new restaurant in new up-and-coming neighborhoods.

- I added time to my schedule to swim every morning and work out my bod. I picked my most muscular friend and hit the gym with him to save the cost of a trainer. I get quality time with him and he gets the benefit of free coaching while we do "crazy eights" weight routines. I am now looking pretty damn good.

- I started taking horseback riding lessons every week with the goal of competing one day. I love being out of my head and connected with the horse. It is so rewarding to bond with such a powerful and intelligent animal.

- I have standing holiday travel plans. I went to Egypt for the holidays last year with my family and we've committed to another trip moving forward. There are so many places to see and foods to experience. I have scheduled all of the different places in the world I want to see. One trip a year in priority of the sites and places I want to experience. I'm off to Australia next on the stock market. I love you Market!

- Mom and I are taking cooking lessons together because I'm a horrible cook. For Christmas I also got my mom and I matching yoga outfits. Because of my career shift I have time to go to classes with my mom, which makes me truly happy. I really want to enjoy her company as much as I can because she means so much to me.

True happiness comes from dreaming and executing your ideal life. You can start dreaming your ideal life when you develop a personal relationship with your money to get you to live it.

You can follow my blog at *iheartmoney.com*. I will be blogging about everything from coaching to saving on everyday purchases to building stock portfolios. My mission is to help people build personal and financial capital, so check back frequently.

And be sure to love your money.

i ♥ money

EXERCISES

For your convenience, I've duplicated the exercises that appear in the pages of the book. Use them here or copy them and use them often. You'll find them helpful in setting and achieving your goals.

Behaviors that Limit Your Wealth

Take out a piece of paper and write down all the things you will be as a rich person.

> *Example:* *Good with money*
> *Saver*
> *Hoard capital*
> *Savvy and wise*
> *Knowledgeable about markets and business*
> *Always learning*
> *Noble*
> *Honest*

Take out a second piece of paper and write down the behaviors you will not have as a rich person.

> *Example:* *I spend more than I make*
> *I owe money*
> *Have credit card debt*
> *No investments or growing assets*
> *Unknowledgeable and poor with money*

Now, strike a line through all of the behaviors you will no longer practice and tear up the sheet of paper. You are now going to think like a rich person, behave like a rich person, and thus live like a rich person. It is never too late to be rich. Why not start right this second? Throw the scraps of ripped up paper out and let them symbolize this moment of your transformation to being a rich person.

Write out what you are going to be as a rich person once a day for 21 days.

EXERCISE 2

Turning Limitations into Empowerment

Write down your limiting belief on a piece of paper.

Example: "I'll have to make new friends if I become rich."

Now cross out this sentence and write after it 25 times:

I deserve to be rich
I am worthy of being rich
I will be rich
I must be rich
I shall be rich
Rich is good

Do this as many times as you need to until you no longer associate with the limiting belief.

Personal, Professional, and Material Goals

You need three sheets of paper.

1. At the top of the first sheet write "Personal Goals."

    Brainstorm everything that you want to accomplish in your life that is of personal importance. This includes relationships you want to have or improve, educational programs, volunteering and philanthropic work, and physical challenges you want to accomplish, like yoga or an Iron Man competition.

    Think big—this is your life!

    Do not hold anything back. Let it all flow out and fill as many pages as you can, even if you feel yourself doubting anything on the list. Write down everything.

2. At the top of the second sheet write "Professional Goals."

    Now do the same thing. Open the floodgates and brainstorm every possible thing that you want to achieve in your career. Again, do not limit yourself. You are your best champion so write down everything you want to achieve. Write down if you want to change careers at a certain point in time, if you want to start your own business, go into politics, work abroad, anything that you can dream of.

    I can dream a lot so my goals folder is hefty and yours should be too.

3. At the top of the third sheet write "Material Goals."

    This is the fun one for me. Anything that you want to buy goes on this one: trips to Europe, luxury cars, art, diamonds, whatever your heart desires.

Now that you have all of your hopes and dreams brainstormed, we are going to add them to your own personal "Life Status."

LIFE STATUS: Personal Goals

Goal	Description	Value	Priority	Due Date	Current Status	Next Step	Cost

LIFE STATUS: Professional Goals

Goal	Description	Value	Priority	Due Date	Current Status	Next Step	Cost

LIFE STATUS: Material Goals

Goal	Description	Value	Priority	Due Date	Current Status	Next Step	Cost

EXERCISE 4

Your Core Values

To determine your core values, take out a pad of paper and pen. Think of people in your life or from history who have characteristics that you respect.

Now, think of what specific characteristics you admire and write them down for each of the individuals that you picked.

Look at the characteristic of each character. There should be 8-10 character traits.

Now ask yourself, if you had that character trait, what values would you really possess?

> *Example:*
> *Julius Caesar is someone from history that I respect. I like that he was ambitious (to say the least). If I had Caesar's ambition, what would I have? I would have success. And if I had success, what would I have? I would have confidence. And if I truly felt confident, what sense would I have? When I think long and hard about it, I would have a sense of achievement.*

That exercise showed that one of my core values is achievement.

Exercises

EXERCISE 5

Your Perfect Money Match

On a piece of paper, describe how your perfect money match is with money. Consider these points:

How much do they make?

_____

_____

_____

_____

_____

Are they frugal but not cheap?

_____

_____

_____

_____

Are they generous to the people they really love?

_____

_____

_____

_____

_____

How do they spend their money and what value does it bring them?

_____

_____

_____

_____

_____

What kind of ambitions do they have?

_____

_____

_____

_____

_____

Describe them on paper to fit your vision of your perfect money match. Like a lighthouse, you'll beam this ideal out when dating and you'll quickly attract these types. You'll also instantly see if someone is not up to par.

GLOSSARY

401(K) – A retirement plan in which contributions are on a pre-tax basis. With either pre-tax or after-tax contributions, earnings from investments in a 401(K) account (in the form of interest, dividends, or capital gains) are tax deferred. The resulting compounding interest with delayed taxation is a major benefit of the 401(K) plan when held over long periods of time.

ADVISOR – Someone who gives financial advice and buys and sells financial products for clients. Also known as Stock Broker, Financial Planner, Investment Advisor.

ASSET – Something you own that has a value if sold, like property, cars, stocks, bonds, mutual funds.

BOND – A debt investment with which the investor loans money to an entity (company or government) that borrows the funds for a defined period of time at a specified interest rate.

BROKER – Someone who gives financial advice and buys and sells financial products for clients. A party that mediates between a buyer and a seller. A broker who also acts as a seller or as a buyer becomes a party to the deal. Also known as an Advisor, Financial Planner, Investment Advisor.

BROKERAGE – A "brokerage" or a "brokerage firm" is a business that acts as a broker.

BUDGET – An estimate, often itemized, of expected incomes and expenses for a given period in the future.

CHECKING ACCOUNT – A bank deposit against which checks can be drawn by the depositor.

COMMISSION – A fee charged for a service rendered. The fee they charge when you buy or sell a stock.

CORE VALUES – Represent an individual's highest priorities and deeply held driving forces.

COMPOUNDING INTEREST – *Interest* is added to the principal, so that from that moment on, the interest that has been added also itself earns interest.

CONTRIBUTION – Money directed into any government sponsored account such as an IRA, Roth IRA, 401(K), Roth 401(K), or ESA.

CONTRIBUTION MATCHING – When an employer matches, to some level, the amount you personally directed into a savings plan, a 401(K) is typical.

CREDIT BALANCE – The amount remaining on a credit card account that an individual must still pay for.

DEBT – An amount owed to a person or organization for funds borrowed. Debt can be represented by a loan note, bond, mortgage or other form stating repayment.

DISTRIBUTIONS – The money a stock, income trust, index or mutual fund will pay out on its unit or to its shareholders.

DIVIDENDS – Payments made by a corporation to its shareholder members. It is the portion of corporate profits paid out to stockholders.

DISCOUNT BROKERAGE – A business that charges clients significantly lower fees than traditional brokerages, typically offering comparatively fewer services and/or support.

DOLLAR COST AVERAGING – An *investment strategy* designed to reduce *volatility* in which *securities*, typically *mutual funds*, are purchased in *fixed dollar amounts* at regular *intervals*, regardless of what direction the *market* is moving. Thus, as prices of securities rise, fewer *units* are bought, and as prices fall, more units are bought.

DIVIDEND RE-INVESTMENT PLAN (DRP) – Plans that re-invest dividends paid to buy more of the paying companies' stocks. Instead of being paid in cash, you receive more shares in the underlying company.

DRP – See Dividend Re-investment Plan.

DEPOSIT – Something that is owed or that one is bound to pay to or perform for another.

ETF – See Exchange Traded Fund.

EXCHANGE TRADED FUND (ETF) – A fund that is traded on a stock exchange.

EQUITY – Stock or any other security representing an ownership interest.

FIXED INCOME – Gaining or yielding a more or less uniform rate of income from a bond or other financial product.

FIXED COSTS – Expenses that are constant for a company or person no matter what the production level is, e.g. rent.

FIXED RATE – A rate (as of interest) that stays the same.

GROWTH RATE – The annual rate at which a variable, such as a firm's earnings, has been or is expected to grow. One common method of estimating future growth rate is simply to measure a variable's past growth rate and then project a continuation of the trend.

HOLDINGS – Legally owned property, such as land, capital or stocks. Often used in the plural.

INCOME FUNDS – An income fund is a mutual fund whose goal is to provide an income from investments.

INDEX – In the case of financial markets, an index is essentially an imaginary portfolio of securities representing a particular market or a portion of it. Each index has its own calculation methodology and is usually expressed in terms of a change from a base value. Thus, the percentage change is more important than the actual numeric value.

INTEREST – The charge for the privilege of borrowing money, typically expressed as an annual percentage rate.

INVESTMENTS – The investing of money or capital in order to gain profitable returns, as interest, income or appreciation in value.

LIABILITIES – Moneys owed; debts or pecuniary obligations as opposed to Assets (see above).

MANAGEMENT FEES – Periodic payment that is paid by investors in a pooled investment fund to the fund's investment advisor for investment and portfolio management services.

MANAGED FUNDS – Refers to a *portfolio management* strategy where the manager makes specific investments with the goal of outperforming an investment benchmark index.

MARKET – Typically refers to the equity market where stocks are traded, but can also refer to the bond, options or commodity market.

MANAGEMENT EXPENSE RATIO (MER) – The ratio of the inherent costs incurred in operating a unit trust fund to the fund's average net asset. MER allows unit holders and investors to make direct comparisons of the costs carried by competitor funds of the same fund categories/peer, e.g. between one balanced fund and another.

MER – See Management Expense Ratio.

MUTUAL FUNDS – A mutual fund is a professionally managed collective investment scheme that pools money from many investors and invests it in stocks, bonds, short-term money market instruments.

NET WORTH – The total *assets* minus total outside *liabilities* of an individual or a *company*.

OVERDRAFT – The amount by which withdrawals exceed deposits, or the extension of credit by a lending institution.

PLEDGE ACCOUNT – When a loan is secured against a portfolio of investments.

PORTFOLIO – The group of assets, such as stocks, bonds and mutuals, held by an investor.

RETURN – The amount of profit, before tax and after depreciation, made from an investment, usually expressed as a percentage of the original total cost invested.

ROTH IRA – Contributions are made with after-tax assets, all transactions within the IRA have no tax impact, and withdrawals are usually tax free.

ROYALTY TRUSTS – An investment that may hold equities, debt instruments, royalty interests or real properties. Their stated goal is to pay out consistent *cash flows* for investors.

STOCK – A type of security that signifies ownership in a corporation and represents a claim on part of the corporation's assets and earnings.

TRADITIONAL IRA – Contributions are often tax deductible ("money is deposited before tax" or "contributions are made with pre-tax assets"), all transactions and earnings within the IRA have no tax impact, and withdrawals at retirement are taxed as income (except for those portions of the withdrawal corresponding to contributions that were not deducted).

UNITS – A fund is divided into units and each holder is entitled to a proportionate share of the fund. Each "unit holder" has the right to their share of the assets of the fund and any income that the fund earns.

VARIABLE COSTS – Variable costs are expenses that change in proportion to the activity of a business or individual.

VARIABLE RATE – Any interest rate or dividend that changes on a periodic basis. The change is generally related to the Federal Reserve prime lending rate.

YIELD – Describes the amount in cash that returns to the owners of a security.

ABOUT THE AUTHOR

Mr. Lester studied Political Science and Economics at the University of Western Ontario, and International Marketing at Orebro University, Sweden. He completed his professional coach training through Erikson College in Vancouver, B.C. He has worked at Merrill Lynch, BMO Financial Group, and BMO Nesbitt Burns. He has helped a diverse group of people, from high net worth individuals to students, build personal and financial capital.

In 2003, he began to work in advertising and communications. Many of his clients have been large financial institutions, which he has helped by improving their marketing appeal to everyday people.

He is now a professional Financial Coach, and President of DCL Capital Holdings Inc. Lester writes for his blog *iheartmoney.com* that breaks with traditional attitudes towards finance, and describes his own philosophy towards money and life that he has gained through his personal and professional experiences. His philosophy on money applies to many areas of everyday life including: banking, investing, goal setting, shopping, and entertainment.